A DENTIST'S BLUEPRINT
TO SUCCESS

All Dental Offices Are Not Created Equal

The Step-by-Step Process to Owning Your Own Dental Office and

Making Your Dream a Reality!

Steve Anderson

Copyright © 2017 Steve Anderson
All rights reserved.
ISBN: 1542361532
ISBN-13: 978-1542361538

CONTENTS

Foreword by Dr. Ash Kaushesh	i
Acknowledgements	ii
Introduction	iii
Your Vision	1
Preparing for Your New Office	5
Selecting Your Dental Team	7
Counting the Costs	28
How Big Do I Make My Office?	33
Selecting an Office	35
Flow & Design	43
The Architectural Plans	48
Material Finishes	50
Construction Costs	52
Contracting with a General Contractor	56
Timelines for Your Project	61
The Flow Chart	63
The Business Model	67
Planning the Move	69
Celebrate Your Opening	73
Additional Helps	74
Office Maintenance	83
Case Studies	87
Wrap-Up	93
What Clients Have to Say	95
What Lenders Have to Say	98
Special Thanks	99
About Steve Anderson	100

FOREWORD

The manuscript you are holding in your hand is the very first of its kind. This set of documents hold the key to unlock the potential for a new beginning for any dentist. It is the exact turnkey methodology that has been missing from the profession. Steve Anderson has filled the voids between dreams and reality.

First, a little about the author. The first time I shook hands with Steve he impeccably asked every question to get to know my style of practice and what makes me tick. The second time I met with Steve and saw the way he worked, he personified every expectation from a client. His work area is the most organized I have ever seen and is full of colors, sticky notes and diagrams. Steve doesn't miss any details. What is important to his client is important to him. But his professionalism goes above and beyond pleasing the client. His level of belief and the trust him and his client share reaches further than just being on time and always having impeccable communication. That Professionalism and trust enables him to guide the client in the right direction towards success and he is not afraid to speak his mind about what truly benefits the situation.

The manuscript you hold is a summation of every office Steve has helped build, every client he has helped from the ground up, and every hand he has shaken and learned from throughout his professional life.

The amount of detail in this manuscript is mind-boggling, yet concise and accurate. I find myself reading and re-reading every page multiple times because it cuts to the heart without the fluff. I find myself admiring his courage to address the complexities of what it takes to be successful in building, opening, and maintaining a successful and ethical dental business model. The amount of subjects - from describing the business model, true and tested, to maintenance schedules of equipment is a lifeboat, a raft, a propelled jet and a rocket at the same time, depending upon how the beneficiary decides to grasp and apply the material.

The design of the manual can easily be followed. It hits the most important points like a hammer to a nail. What is remarkable is that it empowers the reader and helps them find their inner voice. Most of what is written is not only intuitive but also encouraging. After having built numerous offices and helping many doctors over the years myself as a practice consultant, I find this work to offer knowledge and wisdom that flows from Steve's heart and a relentless pursuit for perfection and truth. In a nutshell, I find it to be an honest and reliable teacher and mentor for any new starting dentist. I applaud Steve for his effort and integrity.

Ash Kaushesh DDS, MAGD, MaCSD, DDOCS, DABOI/ID
Master of the Academy of General Dentistry
Master of the College of Sedation in Dentistry of the American Dental Society of Anesthesiology
Diplomate of the Dental Organization for Conscious Sedation
Diplomate of the American Board of Oral Implantology/Implant Dentistry

ACKNOWLEDGMENTS

Two major events were instrumental in making this book happen, the 2008 market crash and the ensuing challenge to re-invigorate the dental market. Marty Fifer, AIA; his associate, Casey Potash; and I teamed up in late 2009 to create a presentation to stimulate the dental market. I am so thankful for them both, their enthusiasm and passion for the dental market!

These catalysts invigorated me to take my compilation of notes and comments of 10 years and create the beginning of what you see today!

I am so blessed to have been around so many insightful, knowledgeable and helpful people! Thank you to the many friends, family and professionals that made a difference for me and unknowingly impacted the contents of this book. Please take a moment to see a more comprehensive list at the back of this book.

I also want to thank my wife, Debbie of 38 years who continues to challenge me to do my best, desires that I do what I enjoy, who puts up with my new endeavors, and helps soften my rough edges. I love you, Debbie.

Steve

INTRODUCTION

CONGRATULATIONS!

If you are reading this, it means you have taken the first step toward your future new office or remodel. It is our desire to share with you our knowledge and experience in selecting the Team of Experts that will build your office and provide you with the tools beneficial to save you time, money and effort as you Make Your Dream a Reality!

If you want to save time, money, effort and understand the process of *Making Your Dream a Reality* by owning your own dental office, this book is for you. It is designed to take anywhere in the world and provide simple easy to use principles and forms to Make Your Dream Reality!

When I chose to specialize in dental construction in 1997, a common topic among clients was "What do I do first…" or "…where do I begin?" with most of the comments coming from recent graduates.

This started a compilation of notes, comments, thoughts and ideas of what it takes to get a dental office started while making the best decisions possible along the way.

This book has been used and shared with hundreds over the past 8 years, in college lectures and training, and dental seminars. All of the forms, charts, bullet points and helps were a result of conversations I have had with dentists over the years and my own personal growing experiences, many of which were painful and expensive.

My hope is that you, the dentist, will be kept from dealing with issues that I and many others have had to endure and overcome, such as purchasing items you do not need or will not use, paying large sums of money for services that are not needed, paying 2 or 3 times for things, having an office over or under built, ending up with an office that you do not like, and so on!

How do you do this? By reading the simple step by step processes contained within this book. You will learn that it is ok to say "NO", how to find and surround yourself with the best professional team, the sequential process to create your dream office, establish your vision, a budget and what it includes, find the best office negotiator for your space many times for free, get the best office negotiated at the best price, and so much more!

Please note that the Contents page has listed each chapter in order of what I believe to be the most productive and efficient as a dentist begins and works through their dream of owning a business.

You will notice that introductory narratives are left out as this book was first designed as an aide for my lectures and seminars that are 1 to 4 hours long. My hope and desire is to complete and update this book with important additional insights and changes in the market place that I have learned most recently.

INTRODUCTION

This book is designed to be used anywhere in the world. However, it is important to rely on strong, trusted team members as local codes, processes, and requirements by municipalities and jurisdictions often differ. Some may not require permits, others may not require architects, while others may not require General Contractors. This is all the more reason to find that trusted team member to aide in your future!

I have always had a deep desire to help others and make a difference. The only regret I have is not publishing this when I completed it nearly 8 years ago. I hope and pray that this book will be a gift of knowledge to simplify and ease the process of *Making your Dream a Reality!*

DREAMS DO COME TRUE...
May this be your first step!

Steve Anderson
President
Denco Dental Construction, Inc.

1
YOUR VISION

SEMINAR IMPLEMENTATION NOTES

Successful Project Attributes

Date to Complete	Action Point/Contact	Issue/Item to Work On

Developing "The Plan"

Some Simple Business Questions to Ask Yourself

- What type of dental practice do I want to have?
- Where do I want to live and work?
- Do I want to be an owner?
- Do I like to make decisions?
- Do I like to work with others?
- What are my weaknesses?
- What are my strengths?
- Do I like to manage others?
- How well do I delegate?
- What will I do to improve my skill sets?
- How big of an office do I want?
- Insurance or fee based service, or mixture?
- When do I want to open my practice?
- What is my Practice Philosophy/Mission Statement? (How will I run my business?)
- What objectives/processes are important to me?
- Goals for my Practice (List quantitative measurable goals with time frames)
- The "Must Haves" in my new office
- The "Would Be Nice to Haves" in my new office?

Describe My Patient Base:

- Demographics
- Income
- Services
- Rendered
- Age
- Gender
- Culture

What will my patients expect from me?

- Quality of service
- Type of services
- Fees
- How much will they expect to pay
- How will they pay (treatment plans, insurance)

What are my personal goals for one year?

Three Years?

Five Years?

Ten Years?

What are my professional goals for one year?

Three Years?

Five Years?

Ten Years?

What types of patients do I want to attract to my practice?

- Type of cases?
- Demographics?
- Revenue?
- Culture?
- Fee structure?

What will my ideal patient expect from me?

- Fees?
- Office atmosphere?
- Treatment(s)?
- Hours of operation?

What is my "Exit Strategy"?

What type and how many team members do I intend to employ?

- Abilities/Talents
- Education
- Titles
- Personality
- Income
- Benefits
- Hours
- Work Ethic

NOTES:

2
PREPARING FOR YOUR NEW OFFICE

BUYING, LEASING, OR BUILDING A NEW OFFICE?

• GET READY – PROPERLY PREPARE	• PRE-QUALIFY	• EVALUATE OBJECTIVELY
• SAVE MONEY – NO BIG PURCHASES	• COUNT THE COST	• BUSINESS PLAN
	• DETERMINE YOUR NEEDS	

Here are some things to consider before taking the plunge.

1. Get Ready – properly prepare. Polish up your credit report: The higher your FICO score, the better. Check out Experian®, Equifax®, or Transunion® to verify reporting is accurate. If there is a late payment history or other credit issue, be sure all accounts are made current and write a letter of explanation regarding payment issue.

2. Save Money – Do not buy big-ticket items such as a house, rental, etc., until you have qualified for a loan. Doing so could hurt your immediate plans as far as lenders are concerned.

3. Down Payment – Rates are down, but in some cases down payment requirements are higher. So investigate and then save for the down payment. Note: Some lenders will lend up to 100%.

4. Pre-Qualify – Start talking with a lender now to see where you stand, what you can qualify for, what areas you should work on, and what advice they have for you.

5. Determine your Needs – Have professionals help you determine the size of office, design level, IT and equipment needs, etc., that you will require.

6. Count the Cost – Make sure you have someone help you determine what all of the costs are going to be. Do a "performance check" to determine what all of your monthly fees, maintenance fees, and other expenses will be. Determine how much will be "out of pocket." Allow for surprises in your budget.

7. Evaluate the Office – Do a building inspection to evaluate access, parking, structural, power, mechanical needs, etc. Inspect and evaluate logistics, dental and patient visibility, and review location, location, location!

8. Evaluate Objectively – Do so with no emotional attachment. Put a package together with the pros and cons, costs, (gross income and approximate monthly expenditures). Sit down with your spouse, a close friend, or successful dentist and discuss your project. Does it make sense? Are there any red flags? If there are red flags, pay attention to them!

9. Personal Cash Flow Needs – Determine all your liabilities and break out your monthly lump sum expenses.
10. Broker Lending – Charges a broker's fee for finding you funding. If you find a direct source of funding you avoid extra fees.
11. Financials – Typically lenders will require submission of personal (and business, if applicable) tax returns and a current Year-to-date Profit and Loss Statement (if applicable) on the business.
12. Business Plan – Set your goals, objectives with accountable and measurable steps to aide in your success.
13. Resume/Biography/Schooling – Gather this data and keep up to date.

SUCCESSFUL PROJECT ATTRIBUTES:
- **STRONG TEAM**
- **BUSINESS PLAN**
- **EFFICIENT LAYOUT**
- **SITE SELECTION**

3
SELECTING YOUR DENTAL TEAM

UNDERSTAND:

You cannot do everything yourself and expect to know everything there is to do or what is required.

Whether starting, expanding, remodeling or upgrading your practice, managing a large project can distract a doctor from staying focused on clinical productivity and office efficiency.

To avoid unnecessary pitfalls, it is imperative that doctors surround themselves with a team of experienced experts who understand the business of running a professional practice, the capital investment that is required to enter into ownership, and what it takes to continue dental growth throughout their career.

Benefits of a Solid Team:

- Balanced Life
- Better Time Usage/Management
- Less Stress
- Budget Maintenance
- Fewer Heartaches
- Peace of Mind/Better Overall Health
- Confidence in Things not Over Looked
- Confidence in your Goals
- Confidence in your Outcome
- Confidence in your Team

Remember...

IT'S ALL ABOUT YOU!

As you meet with these professionals, make sure they are listening to you as you share your Dream! This is when it is important to be selfish: Make sure that the professional is all about *your* success and not theirs!

A Balanced Life

- Family
- Social
- Spiritual
- Emotional
- Financial
- Profession
- Physical
- Fun & Recreation

You don't have to know everything...
SURROUND YOURSELF WITH ACCOUNTABLE PROFESSIONALS WHO ARE MORE KNOWLEDGEABLE THAN YOURSELF.

THE TEAM APPROACH

The Team Approach is the most successful way to accomplish your dream. By carefully selecting each professional and involving each one in sharing your dream (and collectively when possible) the most time, money, and effort are saved with the fewest mistakes, problems, duplications, and delays while creating the office of your dreams! Below are the areas of professionals and in priority of when to engage them:

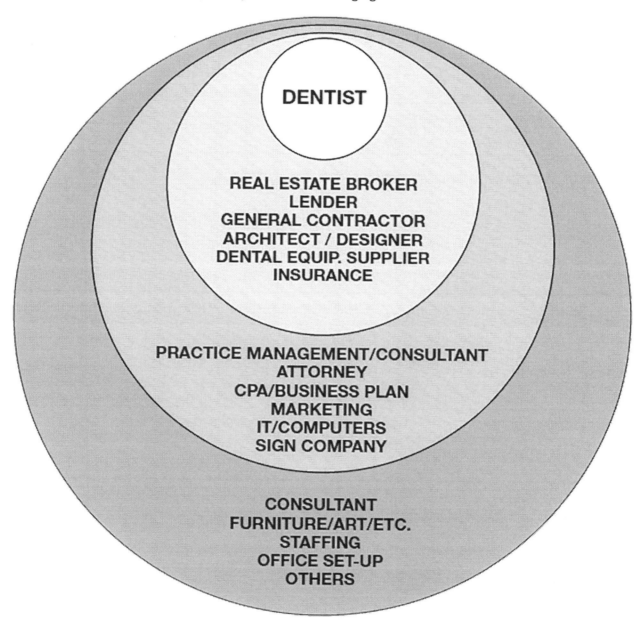

"Surround yourself with quality people, for it is better to be alone than in the presence of bad company." – **George Washington**

THE TEAM GOAL:

- Should be all about your success and making your dreams reality within your stated boundaries.

General Questions When Choosing a Team Member:

- Do they ask proactive or reactive questions?
- Are they listening?
- Do they apply what they hear?
- Are they working for your best interest?
- Are they knowledgeable in dental design and construction?
- Do they give you options?
- Do you connect with them?
- Can you trust them?
- Do they bring synergy to a team?
- Are they open about the costs or are the costs hidden?
- Do you enjoy working with them?
- Do you have references who will vouch for these characteristics?

General Requirements of a Team Member:

- To look for and surround yourself with accountable people more knowledgeable than yourself
- Dental savvy: must understand dentist's needs
- Must operate in the dentist's best interests, both functionally and economically
- Must listen and apply: Every dentist operates differently, so the design should be different
- Should not be a "yes man": must be willing to give trustworthy advice when necessary
- Understand change and the benefits of change
- Understand the "philosophy" of the Doctor, Owner, Manager or Practice clearly through example
- Provides proof of success in the areas of work they represent
- Has integrity in business choices/philosophies with proven examples in work and relationships

- Does not mind potential for conflict in opinions between each other with the understanding that a difference of opinion can be considered an asset
- Understand the challenges of the client as well as the work to be accomplished
- Has a positive and realistic attitude about business
- Promotes positive energy about them that smells like work ethic
- Do they motivate people around them?
- Have they proven you to be trustworthy?
- Are their communication skills a parallel to the client
    - Listening skills proven?
    - Attentive and engaged listeners?
    - Clear and concise?
- Are they able to accommodate various client personalities?
- Do they understand the meaning of time?
- Are they willing to collaborate and listen to input from other experts?
- Check their references. What do your peers say about them?
- Do they follow up?
- Do they meet deadlines?
- **Do you enjoy working with them?**

YOUR DENTAL TEAM — ADVISORS/EXPERTS

	Function	Importance
Realtor	• Evaluates, advises, and negotiates spaces that is best suited for dentist within his budget • Assists with due diligence • Can review lease and purchase agreements. • Can advise and provide suggestions	• Negotiation knowledge, experience, and information is invaluable • Experts at negotiation • Save you time and money • Consults and advises what would be best for you
Lender	• Provides funds for project • Establish loan value and guidelines • May provide other resources and tools to aid in your business success • Can verify neighborhood comps and locality of existing dental offices	• Funds Project • Provides financial program that best fits your needs • Verifies needs of your practice at new location
Architect	• Evaluates programs, designs • Create your new office to meet your vision and goals while adhering to local code guidelines • Verifies square footage of space needed • Creates concepts and specs	• Creates an office that fits your tastes and needs • Maximizes flow and increase productivity. • Advises and evaluates selected building sites
Interior Design/ Decorator	• Assists in selecting finishes such as, flooring, colors, décor, fixtures, art work, furnishings, etc.	• Verifies finishes are appropriate for dental offices
General Contractor	• Create and evaluate a budget • Creates a team and builds your office within your budget constraints and time line • Recommends suggestions to maximize or improve desired intent	• Builds your office • Keeps project within budget • Protects your investment with proper documentation in the field and office that have accountable systems in place • Advise and evaluate selected building sites
Financial Planner	• Evaluates, plans, and advises financial decisions • Can advise on investments and related tax strategies	• Help plans for your future. We recommend starting early and stick to a plan.
CPA / Accountant	• Usually are history gatherers • Evaluates and advises financial decision bases on your history	• Makes sure all taxes and obligations are properly filed • Maximize your office financial procedures
Business Consultant	• Creates a business plan	• Provides a blueprint with important measuring guides establishing your growing business

YOUR DENTAL TEAM — ADVISORS/EXPERTS

	Function	Importance
HIPAA Specialist	• Provides Federal and State compliance to Healthcare Industry laws for your company's protection	• Very important to make sure your office complies with all areas of HIPAA regulation, including recordkeeping
Dental Equipment Specialist	• Evaluates and advises the best choice of equipment and related items for new offices within desired budget • Works with architect to provide all equipment requirements • Advises architect of new office design when applicable	• Makes sure the proper equipment is selected for maximum efficiency and least amount of stress • Can verify what competition, if any, would be in your new area
Attorney	• Reviews lease/purchase documents to ensure client's best interest • Estate/will/employee/partnership planning and documentation	• Acts in your best interest to protect your investments • Verifies that you comply with legal requirements
Marketing Consultant	• Develops marketing plan that creates a brand consistent for all marketing venues • Provides options, budget, and projected results through different mediums	• Helps you identify who you are and create an image/brand • Can maximize dollars spent to draw in new patients
Practice Management Consultant	• Evaluates and helps develop systems to improve and maximize results of office practices (scheduling, patient flow, follow-ups, call-ins, financial arrangements, etc.)	• Can help increase productivity/profits while reducing office stress and turmoil
Insurance Broker	• Evaluates existing coverage • Provides suggestions and options for needed coverage	• Protects your investments by insurance risk and loss potentials
IT Services	• Helps evaluate and determine best options suggestions as they relate to computers, TV's, phones, security, cabling, etc.	• Helps make sure you are up on latest technical options • Saves you time and money by coordinating all required technical items
Sign Company	• Reviews/ evaluates building and city criteria in order to present you with best choices and options for your office • Starts process by the time plans are submitted to the city	• Creates a sign that will attract patients and insure the sign is within code regulations
Mentor	• Considers locating/connecting with a local experienced dentist willing to invest time with you • Can provide valuable advice, ideas, aid in your success, and help avoid pitfalls	• Can provide unbiased knowledge that can save you time, money and problems

YOUR DENTAL TEAM - REAL ESTATE BROKER

Questions to ask the Real Estate Broker

Understand this is the best-kept secret available to you and it is FREE! Even though it is a free service for you, pick the best one available to you! **Keep in mind that this can mean your success...or not!**

- Are they dental savvy? Do they understand the dental business? Are they able to tell you what you will need as it pertains to your office or at least know whom to talk with?
- Are they proactive or reactive?
- Are they knowledgeable? Are they established? Do they know the opportunities available? Are they connected with the market? Do they know how to determine what is a good fit for you or not?
- Do they have similar philosophies as you? Check with their previous dental clients, and see what their comments are. Listen, ask questions, and read between the lines to decipher what is not being said. Ask questions about what kind of dentist to whom you are speaking.
- Go to trusted team members, equipment professionals, architects, contractors, etc. that can steer you in the right direction!
- Do they listen? Do they apply and act on what you say? Do they give you options and support it with good feedback?
- Do they have a reputation for service, results, integrity, disclosure, and transparency?

The biggest mistakes made in Real Estate

- No buyer representation, the doctor tries to negotiate himself
- Only one representative for both sides *Note: There are exceptions to this! When you have a truly committed broker who has integrity and is knowledgeable, one knowledgeable broker can be better than two incompetent ones.
- Not using "dental-minded" brokers

Additional positives

- Comprehensive reports
- Negotiates w/real time history
- Knows the market – who is doing what
- Fees paid for by seller

Remember...

The Real Estate Broker is in the

"DON'T ASK-DON'T TELL" BUSINESS!

...So Ask Questions!

YOUR DENTAL TEAM – Lender

Things to Look for in a Lender...

- Industry and Project Experience -

    A lender should demonstrate a working understanding of the business nuances of a dental practice

- Practice Planning Resources -

    These are useful tools and professional references to assist doctors with their budget and projections.

- Affordable Loan Structures -

    The loan should be structured to include repayment terms that mirror current revenues and anticipated growth.

General Questions to ask the LENDER...

- Are they dental savvy? Do they understand dental operations: the costs, overhead, percentages, etc. needed for excellent advice, consultation and evaluation?
- Have they ever financed a dental office before?
- Which specific markets do they serve?
- May I speak with existing dental customers?
- How does the approval process work?
- Who will fund my loan?
- Who will service my loan?
- Who do I call if I have questions or need help?
- How can they help if I experience problems in my practice now or later in my career?
- Are they proactive or reactive and does this match your expectations?
- Check with their previous dental clients, and see what their comments are. Listen, ask questions, and read between the lines to decipher what is not being said. Ask questions about what kind of dentist to whom you are speaking.
- Discuss and understand what services they provide, what services they recommend and why, and what the fee structure will be.
- Are they aware of all of the "soft costs" involved such as sheet-rock, electrical, plumbing?
- Can they offer you a graduated loan repayment plan?
- How does the disbursement of the funds work?
- Do you have a prepayment penalty?

- Do they fund your loans or is a second party involved?
- What business tools and professional services do they offer to assist dentists?
- Can they help with budgets and projections?
- Do they offer modified loan structures that reflect current revenues with anticipated growth?
- Are they a direct source of funding or a broker? (Brokers have extra fees.)
- Are they around after funding for future needs and questions?
- Ask for and get references.

Remember…

ALL LENDERS ARE NOT EQUAL!

Each one has different specialties in different areas of expertise. Do not assume they will get you approved at their quoted rate.

ASK EXTRA QUESTIONS!

YOUR DENTAL TEAM – Architect

Questions to ask the Architect/Designer:
Experience

How long have they been in business?

- We recommend that they have been working in the architectural industry for at least five years with dental office design experience.
- How many dental offices have they designed?
- They should have designed at least five dental type offices that are similar to your specialty. The requirements and knowledge necessary can vary greatly from one dental specialty to another.
- They should be fully familiar with medical gas systems in addition to underground air and vacuum requirements (NFPA99).
- They should be very familiar with dental office trends that relate to functional, technological and aesthetical needs of dental office design.

Are they a registered licensed architect to practice architecture in the state the project is located?

Does their design team provide interior finish selections from a licensed interior designer? What do these services include? (Interior finishes, lighting, furnishings, window treatments, and special features).

How does the design team provide innovative design solutions that assist dentists with changes in the dental industry such as: technology, space requirements, efficiency, ergonomics, practice management and corporate branding?

Obtain references from at least two dental and two equipment companies.

Design Philosophy/Approach

What is their design philosophy for designing dental offices? How do they design for each client's specific needs?

What is their design process for designing dental offices and how does it differ from other office types? Dental offices require a greater level of detail than most building types due to the specialized needs of:

- Technology requirements
- Equipment coordination and requirements
- Ergonomics of dentistry

What internal design systems does the team have in place to properly communicate each client's specific needs with regard to the engineering, the dental equipment supplier, contractors, IT consultants and city reviewing agencies?

Do they provide different levels of design assuring that the dental office design will meet each client's unique aesthetical goals?

Do they charge differently for a simple dental office design versus an elaborate design?

What tools do they provide (in your base fee) that assist the client in visualizing design options other than the design drawings?

Feasibility Study

Does the firm provide a feasibility study as part of your standard scope of services?

How does the design team determine your needs?

- The design team should provide detailed programming analysis at the beginning of the design process.
- The design team should be providing detailed design options to the dentist throughout the entire design process.

Does their feasibility study verify that the office building will meet the electrical, ADA, mechanical, plumbing, functional, parking, signage and space needs?

Do they field measure the existing space and visit the existing space to become familiar with the existing conditions?

What documents do they need to verify the feasibility? Do they assist in obtaining these documents?

Dental Equipment Experience

What experience do they have working with dental equipment suppliers? Who would they recommend for dental equipment and why?

How do they integrate the dental equipment selection process into their design process?

- Since each piece of dental equipment has specific power and space needs, it is essential that the dental equipment supplier and the design team work together seamlessly throughout the process

Contractor Coordination

Does the firm provide project procurement services in their base fee?

Does the firm assist in sending bid invitations to contractors? Does the firm provide bid comparison services?

Do they provide construction administration services in their base fee?

Do they provide a final walk-through with the general contractor after project completion and provide a written punch list as part of their base fee?

What is their response time to contractors that have questions during construction?

Quality of Documents

Do they provide detailed design documents prior to commencing with engineering? Do they show the dental equipment on the floor plan and in interior elevations?

Do they design and draw cabinets throughout the office that detail all of the following:

- Dental equipment integration?
- Office equipment integration?
- IT and AV systems integration?
- All interior finish requirements?

Do they show sections through the space that depict the design intent? Do they show a detailed finish plan?

How do they depict and select interior finishes that are conducive to dental office use?

Do they show accessory specifications (toilet paper dispensers, keyboard trays, etc.) in their drawings? Does their firm provide design options for window treatments?

Can they provide written testimonials that demonstrate the quality of the firm's design documents?

Design Schedule

Do they provide a design schedule to each client?

How busy is their firm at this time and how quickly can you start on this project? What is the average time frame for design?

What are their turn-around times for: call backs, drawing revisions and design phase? How do their drawings benefit the design, city review and construction schedules?

Cost and Expenses

What and how do they charge?

Do they charge reimbursable expenses above your base fee? Do they provide an allowance or budget for such expenses?

What is the average cost of reimbursable expenses for dental offices of the proposed scope?

Construction Administration

The Architectural Construction Administration is used primarily in very large commercial projects and/or when the General Contractor is a "weak link". The majority of tenant improvement for dental offices do not use this service provided by the architectural team.

By involving a general contractor and an architect/designer that possess good communication skills

- Challenges during construction are minimized by a solid team
- Client time away from office is minimized
- Change orders are reduced/eliminated
- Construction schedule stays on track

Remember…

ALL ARCHITECTS ARE NOT CREATED EQUAL!

Each one has different specialties in different areas of expertise so take time to make sure that they are listening to your desires and that your personalities match as you will be working with them for several months.

YOUR DENTAL TEAM - General Contractor

Questions to ask the GENERAL CONTRACTOR

How long have they been in business?

- We recommend that they have been a general contractor with at least five years dental office construction experience.

Is their general contracting license in good standing?

- You can check this through local licensing boards. Are they licensed in your state and local city/ town?

Do they have a tax number for the city/town that you're building in?

- Most local municipalities require each general contractor to have a city tax number.

Is the general contractor's company in good financial standing?

- Have them send you a list of sub-contractor names with contact information for you to call and ask if they have a good working relationship with the general contractor.
- Check local state sites for any mechanics liens against the general contractor.
- Check the IRS for any liens – contractors have particular tax requirements that can be delinquent at times.

How many dental offices have they built?

- They should have built at least five different dental type offices that are similar to your specialty. The requirements and knowledge necessary can vary greatly from one dental specialty to another.
- They should be fully familiar with medical gas systems, in addition to underground air and vacuum requirements (NFPA99).

What services do they provide as a general contractor that is unique for dental office construction?

- They should be coordinating all dental equipment and cabinet requirements with the dental equipment supplier prior to underground work being completed and throughout the course of construction.
- They should coordinate all cabinet construction requirements with the dentist and dental equipment supplier during the shop drawing process.
- They should coordinate all outlets and switch locations with the dentist and dental equipment supplier prior to applying drywall to the walls.

What Kinds of Insurance should the contractor provide?

- This should be coordinated with your lender, legal counsel and/or insurance company prior to initiating your contract with the landlord.

Obtain references:
- At least five dental clients
- At least two lenders
- At least five vendors/sub-contractors (framing companies, plumbers, blue print companies, painters, etc.)

Who will be their superintendent? How many hours per day will (s)he be at your project? How many projects will (s)he be working on at any given time?
- This will vary depending on the size and complexity of projects that a general contractor has at any given time.
- Do not let the superintendent be "over" worked. They need to give YOUR project the attention that it deserves.

How are they paid? How do they calculate the percentage completed?
- Each state has payment requirements to sub-contractors and vendors that need to be followed. If these laws are not followed, the dentist can be put in a bad legal position. We recommend that this requirement be coordinated with your legal council.
- Most lenders have payment requirements that must be followed. Verify these requirements with your lender prior to signing a contract with your contractor.

How do they pay their vendors and sub-contractors? Do they have procedures that avoid applying liens after payment, while providing accountability to complete their work (through the final punch list)?
- Contractors utilize "Conditional" and Unconditional" waivers to assure payment. We recommend that your legal counsel provide you advice on your state requirements. Lenders also have requirements.
- In the end – IT IS YOUR MONEY SO DO NOT ASSUME THAT IT IS BEING HANDLED BY YOUR CONTRACTOR – KEEP THEM ACCOUNTABLE THROUGH YOUR CONTRACT.

Does the contractor perform a walk-through with the dentist and provide a written punch list of items that need to be corrected prior to final payment?

How does the contractor schedule and charge for special inspections?
- Many local jurisdictions will require the engineer of record, architect of record or a third-party testing agency to perform special inspections. Coordinate this requirement with your architect and contractor prior to commencing with construction.

Does your contractor have any "In-House" trades that will be utilized in the course of construction?

How long has the contractor done business with their vendors and sub-contractors? Have they built dental offices before?

Keep in mind, the general contractor is usually the company performing the work – they monitor the work (in most cases). **The general contractor's sub-contractors and vendors must have extensive dental office experience.**

YOUR DENTAL TEAM – Dental Equipment Specialist

First question and most important
Are they a better listener than a talker?

Second question, similar to the first
Are they here for the quick sale or as a lifetime team member helping to grow the practice? *(In other words, are they going to tell you what you want to hear or the truth!?)*

Experience
How many recessions or downturns in the economy has his/her company been through? How long have they been in business?

- We recommend that the company has been working in the dental industry for at least forty years.
- That way there is a proven track record for a couple of generations of dentists working with equipment in relation to repairs, warranties, service, etc.
- As for the specialist, he/she should have at least five years of dental equipment experience. This will ensure that he/she knows various types and brands of equipment.

How many dental offices have you equipped?

- They (specialists) should have equipped at least twenty dental offices that are similar to your requirements. The requirements and knowledge necessary can vary greatly from one dental office to another.
- They should be fully familiar with medical gas systems, in addition to underground air and vacuum requirements (NFPA99).
- They should be very familiar with dental office trends that relate to functional, technological and aesthetic needs of dental office design.
- They should know equipment requirements and have suggestions that provide solutions for your specific needs.
- They should have options on equipment…from top of the line to value-based lower priced equipment - watch out for simply cheap equipment made with mostly plastic components
- They should know the backing requirements, plumbing requirements, electrical requirements, and technology requirements of all their equipment.
- They should be surrounded by a great team of installers, support personnel and trainers insuring that the job is going to go smoothly.

What experience do they have working with dental contractors and architects?

How does the Dream Team (Equipment Supplier, Architect, Contractor) provide innovative design solutions that assist dentists with changes in the dental industry such as: technology, space requirements, efficiency, ergonomics, practice management and corporate branding?

Obtain references from them - we recommend:
- At least ten dental client references.
- At least two contractor or architect references. Who will be in charge of the project?

Design Philosophy/Approach

Do they work well with the architect on projects?

Do they work well with the contractor on projects?

How many projects has the (Dream Team) worked on together?

Does the design process/dental equipment involve/include the architect (and contractor)?
- Dental offices require a greater level of detail than most building types due to the specialized needs of:
    - Technology requirements
    - Equipment coordination and requirements
    - Ergonomics of dentistry
    - Dental Equipment Specifications
- Since each piece of dental equipment has specific power and space needs, it is essential that the dental equipment supplier and the design team work together seamlessly throughout the process.

Recommendations

We all know that recommending someone is a reflection on ourselves. Our own reputation is at stake here. So, with that being said...

Who would they recommend for a contractor and why? Who would they recommend for an architect and why? Who would they recommend for a banker and why?

Does the Equipment Specialist perform a walk-through with the dentist and provide a punch list of items that need to be corrected?

Does the equipment company provide training on all of the new equipment?

Does the equipment company provide any warranties on the service and the equipment?

Does the equipment company provide a regular maintenance schedule to help you care for your equipment throughout its lifetime?

Is the equipment person surrounded by a complete team of people ensuring that you are going to get taken care of?

YOUR DENTAL TEAM – Attorney/CPA/Business Planner/Consultant

Be clear in what type of service YOU will need.

- Ask what type of services they provide and what they enjoy and excel in providing. Do they align with your needs?
- Have they worked with dentists before and represented them? The importance of this question, on whether or not you hire them, will depend on what services for which you are engaging them.
- Clearly identify your expectations, what they can and will do, and what it will cost. If they utilize an hourly billing system, discuss an average time and a maximum you will allow or have budgeted.
- If you need something that will require more than a few hours to a few days of an investment, ask for references if the attorney was not originally referred, and discuss the attorney's services with the references. Questions to ask: Did the attorney do what (s)he said? Was (s)he accountable? Did (s)he perform, and to what level? Did their bill total what was agreed upon?
- Are they dental savvy? Do they understand dental operations: the costs, overhead, percentages, etc. needed for excellent advice, consultation and evaluation?
- Are they proactive or reactive…and does this match your expectations?
- Do they provide good advice?
- Check with their previous dental clients, and see what their comments are. Listen, ask questions, and read between the lines to decipher what is not being said. Ask questions about what kind of dentist to whom you are speaking. Do they share same philosophies?
- Discuss and understand what services they provide, what services they recommend and why, and what the fees structure will be.

CONSTRUCTION TEAM

If you have already selected a company for the categories listed below, please indicate this by placing an "X" under the "HAVE" column and provide the company/person's name and contact information so we can contact them for scheduling purposes. If you would like us to refer someone to you please place an "X" under the "NEED" column for that category. If an item is not applicable, please list N/A.

Project Name _____

NEED ✖	HAVE ✖	CATEGORY	COMPANY	PHONE	EMAIL ADDRESS
		ARCHITECT:			
		INTERIOR DESIGNER:			
		LENDER:			
		☐ Practice			
		☐ SBA			
		☐ Conventional			
		☐ Business			
		DENTAL EQUIPMENT:			
		Move/Relocate Dental Equipment			
		Disconnect/Reconnect Dental Equipment			
		Chairs			
		Dental Cabinetry			
		X-Ray			
		Pano/Ceph			
		Appraisal of existing			
		Hand piece (sales & repair)			
		ATTORNEY:			
		Business Structure			
		Lease/Contract Review			
		IT:			
		Computer Hardware			
		Computer Software			
		Computer Wiring/Outlets			
		Phone Cabling/Wiring			
		Audio/Speakers			
		Surveillance System			
		Alarm/Security			
		SIGNAGE:			
		Storefront & Monument Signage			
		Temporary Banner			
		Glass/Glazing/Vinyl Lettering			
		MARKETING:			
		Promotional Items			
		Website Design			
		Logo Design/Branding/Corporate ID			
		Printing/Mailers/Door Hangers			
		Special Marketing/Events			
		FURNISHINGS:			
		Artwork/Pictures			
		Furniture			

Project Name:

NEED ✖	HAVE ✖	CATEGORY	COMPANY	PHONE	EMAIL ADDRESS
		CPA:			
		Business Structure			
		Accounting & Taxes			
		CONSULTANT/COACH:			
		Dental Training			
		Dental Referral Marketing			
		Practice Management			
		WATER PURIFICATION:			
		Water Distiller			
		R.O. System			
		MEDICAL GAS:			
		DENTAL PRACTICE:			
		Insurance/Investments			
		Health Insurance & Employee Benefits			
		Insurance Negotiator			
		Payroll, HR and Benefits			
		Chart Filing System			
		STAFFING:			
		Permanent Staffing			
		Temporary Staffing			
		CERTIFIED OSHA TRAINER:			
		DENTAL COLLECTIONS:			
		CREDIT CARD PROCESSING:			
		DENTAL BILLING:			
		SETTING UP OFFICE:			
		Paperwork			
		Forms			
		Insurance Programs for Patients			
		Processes			
		WINDOW TREATMENTS:			
		WALLPAPER NEEDS:			
		WATER FEATURE:			
		Fountain			
		Aquarium			
		Water Wall			
		HIPAA COMPLIANCE:			
		MISCELLANEOUS:			

Revised 1.7.17

4
COUNTING THE COSTS

History of Small Business Success Rates

- 30% of small businesses fail in the first two years.
- 50% of small businesses fail in five years.

Factors:
- Mismanagement
- Poor Business Plans
- Burnout

Reasons Dental Offices Fail
- Wrong loan structure
- High overhead
- Location
- Poor selling practices
- Dentist personality/attitude
- Dentist team personality/attitude
- Technology – needed/not needed/not ready for
- Personal spending – business and personal decisions mixed
- Dentist does not have the 'owner mindset'
- Divorce/personal issues

Good News:
- *Less than .05 % of dental offices failed nationally in 2014.*

The Two Typical Challenges in the New Startup:

- 2-3 years after start – Business is challenging, some slow pays and delinquents, but usually do fine.
- 5-6 years after start – Personnel issues/life issues/marriage/divorce

Now it's time to count the costs:

Does this project make sense? If yes! Go forward with gusto. If not, **Stop**!

Create a compilation budget. See the next page and work with your team of professionals to assist you in creating a budget. Use the projected amount and determine the cost.

*Note: Some items may appear duplicated in different categories. This is in case you outsource the work or do it yourself. This is a brainteaser checklist and may not be exhaustive. If you have any questions, please do not hesitate to call.

You have determined this project makes sense. Involve your lender and make sure you can get a loan for what you want to do. If plenty of money is available, great! If you determined you have a tighter budget, then you need to cut back. **At least you now know what you can qualify for at this stage of your life. This is the size of your dream.** This will help your team know where and how to best help you stay within your budget parameters.

CONSIDER THE BIG PICTURE AND THE ADDED VALUE WHEN MAKING YOUR DECISION.

A THOUGHT...

If you were to spend $10,000 more for something that you really believe in and *increase your productivity by 25-50%* while *reducing stress* and *saving time*, would approximately $60-120/month* be worth the investment?

*Depending on loan rate.

COMPILATION BUDGET

Budget for: Date:

The purpose of this form is to assist you in counting the cost while not overlooking expenses and ensuring your success! Please note that this form was designed for all types of work (ground up, T.I.'s, remodels, etc.). Please be aware that some categories will not apply to you (thus leave them as zero).

In the form, only enter amounts that you want to receive funding.

Projected Amount ($)	Actual Amount ($)	Category
		Building Shell _____ SF
		Land Costs (if separate)
		Tenant Improvement _____ SF
		Tenant Improvement Costs (allowances) for vacancies (if Landlord)
		Contingency - (for unknowns)
		Lease Expenses/Deposits
		Architectural, Permit, City Fees, Designer, and Associated Fees (include fire sprinkler and fire alarm)
		Finance/Loan Costs (If SBA) - Approximate if any (you may want to check with your lender to assist in larger projects and loans)
		Insurance (Check with your lender, several policies usually have to be in place prior to your loan being funded). * Equipment * Practice * Health * Malpractice
		Professional Fees/Services * Designer * Attorney * Consultant
		Signage/Banners
		Utility Fee Deposit * Power * Water * Other
		Working Capital/Start Up Funding *Payroll * Overhead
		Marketing/Advertising/Mailings (some times these costs are part of working capital)
		Dental Equipment * Relocating/ Moving/Set up costs * Gas zone valve * Special Cabinetry (if not part of TI) * Vibrator * Call system * Processor * Dental Chairs * Sterilizer * Doctor stools * Statum * Assistant stools/cart * Autoclave/sterilizer * Delivery units * Air/water separator * Dental lights * Scan X/E-4D/Milling Machines/etc. * Digital radiography * Air Compressor * Recovering of dental chairs * Vacuum * Medical Gas: * X-Ray units * Carts/fixtures/tanks * Pano/Ceph/Cone Beam/etc.

Projected Amount ($)	Actual Amount ($)	Category	
		* I CAT	* Special tables/chairs/equipment
		* Flow meter & bag	* Blanket warmer
		* Gas Manifold w/ switch & alarm	* Lab equipment
		Dental Soft Goods: Merchandise/Hand piece/Etc.	
		* Air abrasion	* Lights: curing & operating
		* Anesthesia equipment	* Lathe
		* Cultura oven	* Model trimmer
		* Dryers, air	* Vacuum former
		* Crown form, bands & shells	* View box
		* Disposables	* Lab monitor
		* Endodontic instruments	* Wall mount delivery
		* Endodontic products	* Trays/cassettes
		* Evacuation products	* Electro surge
		* Finishing & polishing	* Bleaching systems
		* Hand pieces (slow)	* In-office restorative system
		* Hand pieces (hi-speed)	* Cone Beam technology
		* Light/fiber optics	* Acrylics & reline material
		* Impression materials & accessories	* Alloys & accessories
		* Infection control	* Articulating paper & accessories
		* Instruments	* Burs-Carbide & Diamond
		* Laboratory products	* Cements & liners
		* Matrix materials & assoc.	* Cosmetic Dentistry
		* Pharmaceuticals	* Retraction materials
		* Pins & posts	* Rubber Dam & accessories
		* Preventatives & prophy materials	* Sutures & suture needles
		* Lab hand piece	* Uniforms
		* Sandblaster	* Waxes
		* Plaster trap	* Dust vacuum
		* Intraoral/digital cameras	* Plaster pin
		* Ultrasonic cleaner	* X-Ray duplication Cavatron
		IT and Associated Items	
		* Computers: Software/Hardware/Installation	* Networking systems/cabling
			* Security systems/monitoring
		* TV's, monitors, brackets, mounts, arms	* Speakers/sound system
		* Telephone systems	* Cabling
		* Logo/Branding	* Website
		Relocating Moving Expenses:	
		* Movers	
		* Disconnect/reconnect	
		* Phone, IT, Etc.	
		Office Equipment Furnishings/Supplies (Some may be part of TI Expense)	
		* Window treatments	* Chair mats
		* Water feature	* Artwork
		* Wall coverings/faux paint	* Fax
		* Computer installation	* Printers
		* Reception chairs	* Screens
		* Staff room chairs	* Magazine racks
		* Doctor's private office chair	* Fish tank
		* Doctor's private office desk	* Refrigerator
		* Washer/Dryer	* Microwave

Projected Amount ($)	Actual Amount ($)	Category	

		* Waiting room: chairs, rugs, lamps and tables
		* Dispensers: cup/glove/towel
		* Intercom system
		* Copier
		* Open House
		    * Food/drinks
		    * Paper products
		    * Advertising/mailers
		    * Banner
		    * Giveaway/prizes
			* Natural light bulbs
			* Mop/water pail
			* Broom/dust pan
			* Step ladder
			* Vacuum
			* Cleaning supplies
			* RR supplies
			* Break room supplies
			* Clocks
			* Front desk/office supplies

		Total Projected Budget	
		Less Contributions By Landlord/Owner	
		Total	
		Less Personal Investment/Down Payment/Other	
		Total	
		TOTAL TO BORROW	
		Loan #1	
		Loan #2	
		Loan Unfunded	

* Note: Some items may appear duplicated in different categories in case you may hire the work to be done or done yourself.

NOTES:

5
HOW BIG DO I MAKE MY OFFICE?

DENTAL OFFICE PROGRAMMING
General dentist average office square footage (SF)

3 Ops	900-1300 SF
4 Ops	400-1800 SF
5 Ops	1800-2200 SF
6 Ops	2200-2500 SF
8 Ops	2700-3000 SF
10 Ops	3200-3600 SF
12 Ops	3600-4000 SF
18-20 Ops	6000-6400 SF

THE IDEAL SQUARE FOOTAGE:

While the above square footages are typical/average, please note that some locations may require or have available smaller or larger spaces than your program requires (see page 34). Should this happen, be ready to determine:

- What areas are you willing to sacrifice or make smaller should the space be smaller than ideal (i.e., Make the store room smaller or a smaller office or break room?)
- When you have a space that is larger than required, what item in your programing would you add to or make larger (i.e., add an Op, increase a break room, or add a consult room?)

The worksheet on the next page will help you figure out what your square footage needs really are!

SQUARE FOOTAGE NEEDS EVALUATION

Confidential: Yes_____ No _____

Name:	Project Location:
City, State, Zip:	City, State, Zip:

Patients- Avg. Per Day_____ Max Staff: Dr. /Hygiene/Other: _____ #of Doctors & Associates: _____

Qty	Area	Avg. Area	Need	Comments
	Treatment Areas (10x11)	110		
	Surgical Op (14 x 14)	196		
	Pre-Post Op	24		
	Hygiene (8 x 11 or open bay)	88		
	Reception Area (55 sf/station)	110		
	Business Area (40 sf/station)	80		
	File Area	12		
	Waiting Area	185		
	Children's Area	80		
	Consultation Room(s)	90		
	Office Manager	100		
	Sterilization	90		
	Sterile Storage	14		
	Lab	48		
	Separate Milling Area	20		
	Records	60		
	Nitrous Gas Room	10		
	Dark Room	30		
	Panoramic/Cone beam/Ceph/etc.	30		
	Digital Work Area	30		
	Central X-ray Area	48		
	Restroom-Public (ADA)	56		
	Restroom-Staff (ADA)	56		
	Restroom-Doctor (ADA)	56		
	Doctor's Private Office	100		
	Doctor's Offices - Additional	60		
	Lounge/Break room/Laundry	120		
	Storage	30		
	Equipment/Mech. Room	30		
	Wet Storage/W/dryer/Lockers/ChgRm	48		
	Other			
	Subtotal			
	Waste 20% (for hallways)			
	Total			

© 2016 Denco Dental Construction, Inc. Used by permission.

6
SELECTING AN OFFICE

SELECTING AN OFFICE

- What expectations should you have from the broker?
- Dentist self-representation
    - Dentist paying for lease 3 months in advance
    - Only $10/S.F. improvements
- Current leases renegotiated with a dental broker
    - Dentists save $70k over 5 yrs.
- New office negotiations-with dental broker
    - Dentists getting 1.5 Yrs. free rent and $60/S.F. for improvements
- Benefits vary greatly area by area

Biggest Mistake Made by Dentists:

NOT HAVING BUYER REPRESENTATION

Other big mistakes:

Allowing only one broker to represent the seller and the buyer
Not using dental minded brokers

- First start with a real estate representative. He represents you and his fee is FREE, so why not get the BEST one available?

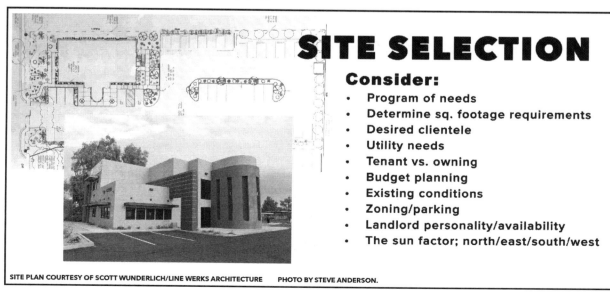

SITE SELECTION
Consider:
- Program of needs
- Determine sq. footage requirements
- Desired clientele
- Utility needs
- Tenant vs. owning
- Budget planning
- Existing conditions
- Zoning/parking
- Landlord personality/availability
- The sun factor; north/east/south/west

SITE PLAN COURTESY OF SCOTT WUNDERLICH/LINE WERKS ARCHITECTURE   PHOTO BY STEVE ANDERSON.

When Doing a Ground-Up Dental Office

Use a Realtor:

When trying to locate a property to build, use a realtor to help locate and negotiate the property.

The Need for a Contractor and Architect:

Once a property is found, take the time to involve your architect and contractor to verify needs and costs that will be associated with the property. Every property is unique and some are more expensive than others when developing. There may be unknown setbacks, underground easements, utility expenses, etc. that can quickly put a project out of reach and/or hurt your future plans.

When selecting a site for your new dental office, we suggest that you coordinate with your architect early in the design and that your architect assist you in obtaining the following information from your real estate professional:

Site Survey (ALTA/Topographical):

Each state has minimum requirements for survey preparation. The purpose of having a good survey done at the beginning is to show existing property lines, easements, site topography, access agreements, trees, buildings, utilities, boulders or outcroppings and any additional existing conditions that will have an impact on your design.

- Note: This document should align with your title report for legal boundaries and information shown within. The site survey will be the basis for the entire design so we recommend that you hire a good surveyor (licensed in your jurisdiction) that provides the highest level of service. Most banks and lenders require an ALTA survey so verify (in writing) specific requirements with each lender.

Environmental Site Assessment:

These studies shall be performed by licensed professionals as early as possible to determine:

1. A historical review of the use and improvements made to the subject property.

2. A review of reasonably ascertainable, practically reviewable, and publicly available building, zoning, planning, sewer, water, fire, environmental and/or other department records.

3. A review of reasonably ascertainable, practically reviewable, and publicly available Department of Environmental Services, Water and Waste Management, Air Quality Division, and (or) other agency records and files.

4. An investigation of the subject property and neighboring properties with regard to the Environmental Protection Agency's (EPA) National Priority List, CERCLA list and similar state lists.

5. An inspection of the site and all improvements with particular attention to the use of hazardous materials in the structures or operating equipment.

6. Verification as to whether present or past owners or tenants have stored, created or discharged hazardous materials or waste, and review of whether appropriate procedures, safeguards, permits, and notices are in place.

7. Each jurisdiction and lender may have specific Environmental Site Assessment requirements so we recommend that you obtain their requirements in writing prior to initiating such studies.

Zoning Information:

Each zoning district has specific requirements and restrictions that may restrict your ability to develop your new dental office design. These requirements may result in:

1. What type of occupancy is allowed, i.e., dental or other professional services.
2. Setback requirements – especially adjacent to residential areas.
3. Parking requirements are usually based on building use. Some jurisdictions may have less stringent parking requirements so we recommend that you base your parking needs according to your office needs as well.
4. Lot coverage restrictions

Local Design Restrictions:

Many neighborhoods and local jurisdictions have a Design Review Board (DRB) or Architectural Review Committees. We recommend that you find out if there are any of the following conditions to your site:

1. Local Design Review Boards: These committees are usually organized by each municipality. They decide on architectural styles, the building forms, building colors and materials, landscape palette and even site design.
2. Covenants Conditions and Restrictions (CC&R) – These documents should be presented to you upon purchasing property and are enforced through architectural committees or associations.
3. Schedule "B" Items in your title report may also outline other design criteria and restrictions.

When You Are 80-90% Sure That the Lease or Purchase Will Go Through…

and while you are finalizing lease/real estate agreement

Start Your Drawings.

BUY VS. LEASE

- Take Time to Compare Options!
- Owning Is Ideal but Not Always Best
- Consider/Compare Investment Required
- Consult Professionals
- Building vs. Buying Risks
- 100% Financing Available

ACQUISITION VS. CONDO TENANT IMPROVEMENT

Acquisition	Condo	Category
$600,000.00	$375,000.00	Building Shell 2,500 SF
$0.00	$0.00	Land Costs (if separate)
$0.00	$275,000.00	Dental Tenant Improvement
$0.00	$0.00	TI Costs (allow.) for vacancies (if landlord)
$0.00	$0.00	Contingency
$0.00	$20,000.00	Architectural/Permit/City Fees
$0.00	$0.00	Finance Costs (if SBA)
$0.00	$0.00	Insurance
$0.00	$0.00	Professional fees/Services
$10,000.00	$10,000.00	Signage Banners
$1,000.00	$1,000.00	Utility Fee Deposits
$0.00	$75,000.00	Start Up Funding (1st Time Dr)
$20,000.00	$20,000.00	Advertising/Marketing
$40,000.00	$175,000.00	Dental Equip, dental soft goods
$5,000.00	$40,000.00	IT & Assoc. Items
$5,000.00	$15,000.00	Office Equip. Furnishings/Supplies
$681,000.00	**$1,006,000.00**	

Dental Office Design Requirements

When leasing or purchasing an existing space, we recommend that the existing facility conditions be reviewed by a registered architect that is familiar with dental office design requirements. Some of the items that the architect should review (but not limited to):

Choosing a Location:
- Patient base
- Referral base
- Marketing
- Signage
- Influences

Building Orientation:
- From best to least desirable: north, then east, then south, and finally west

Site Conditions:
- Does the existing site have adequate parking for dental use in conjunction with existing uses throughout the development?
- Does the existing site have adequate parking for patients and team members that are adjacent to your suite's entrance?
- Does the existing site access meet with local requirements for ADA (Americans with Disabilities Act)?
- Is covered parking offered?
- Signage accommodations
    - Building Signage
    - Monument Signage
- Does the dental office suite have good visibility to attract your patients?

Concrete:
- Does the existing space have an existing concrete slab?
    - If so, was a vapor barrier installed?

Exterior Walls:
- What type of insulation is provided?
- What type of exposure to the sun would you have?

Doors/Windows:

- What type of glass is existing (what is the insulating value)?
- Is the glass tinted?
- What type of sun exposure would you have?
- What type of visibility/views would you have?
- Is there a door for your main (patient) entrance and a private entrance for you and your team? Note: These doors should not be adjacent to each other if you want privacy.
- Does the suite have the required exits per local codes?

Mechanical/Plumbing:

- Does the building and suite have the HVAC system capacity for your heating and cooling needs?
- Does the building and suite have an adequate sewer system for your needs?
- Does the building and suite have adequate water supply (water line and meter) for your dental office needs?
- Is there access to all HVAC and plumbing in above ceiling and floors on multi-level buildings?

Electrical:

- Is the suite metered separately for each tenant?
- Does the suite have adequate power for your dental office needs?
- Is there access to all electrical conditions in above ceiling and floors on multi-level buildings?

Suite Specifications:

- Developer/Landlord TI standards (minimum requirements for improvements).
- Demising wall locations – condo spaces will have a PLAT.
- CC&R document for development
- Maximum ceiling heights

Acquisition vs. Condo

Variables:

- Improvements
- Architect/City permit fees
- Insurance
- Professional services
- Signage
- Utility fees
- Start up funding
- Adversity
- Dental Equipment
- IT, Miscellaneous
- Office equipment/furnishings
- First time/2nd owner
- Monthly payments plus operating expenses if/as applicable

Items to Understand and Consider:

- Count the costs/compare
- Understand all costs
- Patient Files
- Are they real/active?
- What is true value?
- Office status in community
- Why selling?
- Hidden Costs
- Interview Staff
- Ask extra questions
- One Realtor/Professional to represent each side

GREY SHELL

Grey shell space can vary drastically and can greatly impact your tenant improvement costs.

Typically Include:

- Concrete floor
- Demising walls with insulation (no drywall)
- Insulation at the deck
- HVAC penetrations/curb locations (some include units). Typical value of a complete unit is approximately $12,000/unit. There could be warranty issues with the units though.
- Storefront glass and entry
- No power to suite

Typically Do Not Include:

- Concrete (cost approximately $4/SF to complete during TI)
- Demising wall or insulation (can average $3,000/wall)
- No HVAC penetrations/curbs. This necessitates structural engineering and additional framing/roofing.
- Note: Storefront modifications can be expensive.

VANILLA SHELL

Typically Include:

- Concrete floor—no flooring
- Demising walls finished with insulation and the drywall is taped only (typically not textured and painted).
- Grid, tile, and 2X4 fluorescent light fixtures in the ceiling
- Complete HVAC system with thermostat
- Complete handicap restroom- finished complete
- Emergency lighting
- Fire extinguisher

Typical value/cost over a grey shell space is $15-20/SF

- *Note: For most dental offices:
    - A vanilla shell is many times removed. So when you have an option, do not allow them to build a vanilla shell for you.
    - Existing restrooms many times are in the wrong location. Do not let the bathroom location or other existing finishes dictate the design and flow of your office space.

7
FLOW AND DESIGN

PLANNING THE IDEAL OFFICE

Time to think through and evaluate the process. One of the biggest mistakes is not getting a proper flow and design for your new dental office. For instance, leaving a restroom or some existing walls may save only a few thousand dollars, but in the long run result in tens of thousands of dollars in lost production. To demo a suite costs $2-3/SF, but if it is a new office, hire an experienced architect for success. Keep the big picture in mind at all times! This may cost a little more up front, but save thousands in lost production and save you a lot of aggravation.

FUNCTIONAL LAYOUT

Areas to consider:

- **Public Areas - The Three Zones**
    - Waiting
    - Reception
    - Restroom
- **Semi-Public Areas**
    - Operatories
    - Treatment
    - Pre/Post Ops
    - Sterile
    - Lab
    - Consultation Room
    - Records/Diagnostics
- **Private Areas**
    - Private Offices
    - Records/Documents
    - Break Room
    - Restroom
    - Equipment Rooms (mechanical, server, etc.)

Fundamental Layout

Good Flow Practices:

- **Waiting Areas**
    - First impressions, clean, inviting, make it about you and unique
- **Reception**
    - Clutter free, efficient, proper work areas, plenty of check out, all patients visible, split check in and out, greet patients, distance to entry
- **Sterile**
    - Central to operations
    - Location, clutter free, properly sized, efficient, properly zoned, good work areas, good flow, consider equipment when planning
- **Lab**
    - Location not as important as sterile because it's not used as much.
    - Clutter free, properly sized, efficient, good work areas and consider equipment when planning
    - Sit down area needed?
    - Make it a separate room ideally
    - Using carpet tile for the flooring in this area is wise because it keeps the dust to a minimum.
- **Breakroom**
    - No restroom inside the breakroom. Do not use a lab as part of the breakroom work surface. Make a room large enough for team meetings. Next, think about the function of the room and design it to fit your needs.
- **Operatories/Exams**
    - Placement location
    - Set up, design, flow
    - Clean, orderly, clutter-free
    - Flooring
    - Ceilings
    - Technology
    - Entries, openings, open bays
    - Adult areas?

- **Records**
  - More offices are going digital with their records. First determine if this is possible for your office, then determine the location you want to use to store these records
- **Op./Exams Hallways**
  - Design, flow
  - Clean, orderly, clutter-free
  - Flooring
  - Ceilings, add interest
- **Goodbye Area**
  - Consider for patient comfort
  - On way out by check out
- **Equip. Room**
  - Separate room
  - Insulate, hard lid, sound proof, ventilation, keep cool to improve equipment longevity
- **Public Restrooms**
  - Location not in waiting area
  - First impressions are important! Do this room right!
- **Staff Restrooms**
  - Location not in break room, centrally located in the rear hallway
- **Private Restrooms**
  - Locate off private dentist office (shower, other needs)
- **Consult**
  - Important for increasing sales, properly sized, function, needs, dual purpose?
- **Office Manager**
  - Close to front desk and check out, room for small meetings
- **Private Office**
  - Assess your needs, large office for meetings? Small office for only basic work, one or more doctors? Location? Restroom?
- **Pano Area**
  - Ceph, cone beam, technology, separate area, central location, work area needed?
  - The feeling of being radioactively safe

- **Digital Work Area/Order Desk**
    - Functional needs, central located towards rear area or at end of hall? Location in middle?
- **Other Considerations**
    - Add personal touches to make it your own
    - Need a play area?
    - Other special needs required for your office?
    - Walk through your current office and determine what you like/dislike and what you need/do not need

---

OFFICE APPEARANCE FACTS

When the office construction and finishes match who you truly are:

Your performance increases!
Your passion for dentistry comes back!
Your revenue increases!
You will love to come to work!

If you are working in an office that is above or below your desires and expectations:

Your performance struggles!
You have a hard time selling dentistry!
Your revenue and practice struggles!
You have a hard time coming to work!
Eventually you may want to get out of dentistry!

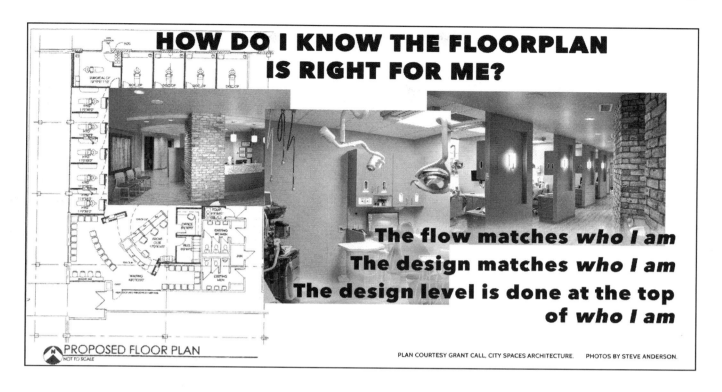

NOTES:

8
ARCHITECTURAL PLANS

Once it's decided that a remodel, tenant improvement or ground-up construction is desired, the architect gets started. Each have their own process, but most importantly involves your dental equipment specialist and contractor in the process to ensure all information gets applied correctly. It is critical early on in your initial floor plan design that you discuss your options with your equipment specialist and contractor. These discussions will include everything **from which your project will be built.**

Be careful to ask questions if you do not know what something means. Make sure your team is doing their part at this stage by providing options, ideas and helping direct you. This is the most important part to **get your dream** in your head **down on paper**.

Schematic Design Notes
It is all about flow and function with your needs
- Floor Plan
- Ceiling Plan
- Power/Plumbing Plan

Design Development Notes
Pay attention to the details

Construction Document Notes
Built from design documents

City Review & Permit Process Notes:
Understand process, length of time and options

"Take time to make sure you have it the way you want it!

Make it Yours, not someone else's!" – Steve Anderson

Architects, Interior Designers, Draftsmen, Equipment Specialists & Interior Decorators

There are many differences among architects, interior designers, draftsmen, equipment specialists and interior decorators, each having their own special place in designing an office. It will depend upon the area of the country, local codes, and what you are needing and/or desiring the outcome of your project to be. Most areas of the country, especially in metro areas, require an architect. Some areas many not require an architect and all of the design work may be handled by an equipment person and a draftsman engaged to get you a space plan. If you are someone with no imagination or who does not have the ability to foresee or understand what you would like your office to be like, you might want to engage in an interior designer. If you are one that only needs help with the colors and basic design, it might be an interior decorator that you engage. All of the professions are important, but not all are usually required to create your new office.

A Summary of Differences in the Different Professions:

Architect:

The architect goes through a rigid schooling process and each typically have their own design and flavor.

They have vast and complete knowledge of what it will take to create your office. They will charge considerably more for it, but a good architect is very worth every penny. They are usually experts in understanding site design, local codes, proper interior design/flow, exterior design, MPE systems, fire protection/alarm systems, submits and obtains permits.

Interior Designer:

The interior designer understands commercial applications and usually has formal training. They are experts in commercial interior finishes, interior office planning, interior lighting, furnishings, art, decor, proper planning, the construction process, and finish/millwork programming.

Drafter:

The drafter usually employed by the architect, but may be independent. They may have a basic understanding or they might actually be a graduate from architecture college. A drafter's expertise can range from someone with the merely the ability to draw to a professional with nearly the full-understanding of an architect.

Interior Decorator:

The interior decorator may have formal training or maybe just learned in the field. Their expertise is usually considerably more limited than that of an interior designer. They excel with artwork and decor selections and design.

9
MATERIAL FINISHES

What phase of design should the interior finishes be selected?

Option 1: During the Design Development Phase
Pros:
- Integral with the architectural aspects
- Hard bids can be completed earlier
- Easier to compare bids when it is competitive bid process
- Finishes with long lead times can get ordered on time

Cons:
- Finishes could be discontinued by the time your project is in construction
- May have to reselect if budget needs to be reduced
- Increases the time it takes to complete the construction drawings, thus adding more time to the schedule

Option 2: During City Review Phase
Pros:
- Utilize the time that the project is in city review, thus reducing the overall design time necessary upfront
- Do not have to reselect if budget dictates "value engineering"
- Reduces the risk of selecting products potentially becoming discontinued (as the order will occur within weeks of selection)

Cons:
- May be limited on selections (i.e.- products that have long lead times)
- Selecting contractor based on allowances without final finish budgetary numbers

Commercial Interior Finish Selections

The Pitfalls of Selecting Your Own Finishes

So many people spend months working with their architect to design a state of the art dream office. Then, somewhere along the process, they attempt to save money by selecting their own finishes. After all, they already know what colors they like…why hire someone to help them? Or perhaps even more common we will hear "I have a friend that can help me…they are really great with color." Reasons why selecting your own finishes is not ideal include:

Color:

When a space is designed by an interior designer, they are looking at the entire project in three dimensions. Color is very important and affects the way the project is perceived. Interior designers have received extensive training to use color as a means to evoke atmospheric ambience and emotion in terms of three-dimensional space. This greatly enhances the architectural design not to mention the unforgettable experience everyone will have when in your office. Not only does color enhance the design, but it will enhance, your, the patient and the staff moods.

Codes:

In commercial spaces, the design and specifications must adhere to certain building codes. A good design team is very educated on local, national, and international building codes. They are constantly keeping themselves up to date on the building codes so that their specifications do not create issues with the governing agencies; this also ensures that your investment is spent wisely.

Durability:

Offices can be designed properly by using timeless and durable products. If done correctly, not only will your office appear to maintain modern standards, but the products used will provide longevity. This can be prevented by working with a design firm that specializes in designing commercial office space and can specifically analyze the durability of proposed specifications. A sign of an experienced design firm is when they maintain a complete design library, full of different levels of commercially acceptable finishes. A designer should work with clients to select appropriate finishes that portray the "timeless" look desired. By "timeless"- we mean the office will continue to look great for years to come, and not just the first month the office is open for business.

Functionality:

An interior designer should analyze what a client will be doing in specific areas and recommend different solutions that will also function well for their use. We have encountered many situations in which the materials were utilized inappropriately due to client unawareness. Make sure the designer is aware of your specific needs for each area of the space.

10
CONSTRUCTION COSTS

THE FOLLOWING FACTORS WILL DETERMINE YOUR CONSTRUCTION COSTS:

- Square footage (size of the office): Generally, the larger the office space, the less expensive per square foot the office construction costs will be.
- Current Pricing of Materials: Construction costs can vary depending on the simple supply and demand for construction materials in specific local economic conditions.
- Complexity of Details: The level of interior architectural design and complexity will significantly dictate the construction costs.
- Level of Final Finishes: The construction costs can significantly vary depending on the exterior and interior finishes.
- Amount of Cabinetry (Millwork): Custom cabinetry can be extremely expensive. Purchasing pre- fabricated dental cabinet units can save on the construction costs but will add to the overall project costs. Tax depreciation should also be considered with your accountant.

COSTS
VS.
SIZE OF OFFICE:

The smaller the office the higher the cost per square foot.
Typically, the larger the office the less cost per square foot.

DENTAL OFFICE SIZE
VS.
COST PER SQUARE FOOT:

Typically, the *lower* the square footage, the *higher* the cost per square foot and vice-versa; when the square footages are higher the cost per square foot will *generally* be lower!

General Contractor Typical Project

Inclusions & Exclusions

Scope of work for general construction on a tenant improvement project typically covers all work and improvements per plans and specs from initial demolition to final inspection. Covered under this scope are all drywall work, plumbing, electrical, mechanical, cabinetry, flooring, and electrical fixtures. Basically all fixed items are included. Additional inclusions typically consist of:

Miscellaneous Inclusions:

- Fire extinguisher(s)
- General liability insurance
- Project coordination and supervision
- Clean up and haul off all debris
- Dumpster and dump fees
- Project detailing
- Sales Tax
- One year warranty

Typical Exclusions:

- Architectural or engineer drawings, city approved plans, blueprints or permit fees or associated costs
- Hook up, installation or relocation of equipment, appliances, fixtures, furnishings, filing cabinets or art work
- Security systems, sound systems, telephone systems, computer systems, paging systems, TV's, mounting and cabling of them or their installation
- Utility or development associated fees/deposits
- Window treatments, wall paper, special wall finishes or their installation
- Equipment insurance
- Exterior signage, numbering or its installation
- Telephone demarc runs
- Performance and payment bonds
- Wiring, hookup and/or installation of equipment provided by others
- Surveying fees and/or demising wall placement

Additional Exclusions That May Occur:
- Fire alarm drawings, fire sprinkler drawings
- Fire alarm system
- Fire sprinkler system
- Water feature/special art or building construction features
- HVAC third party testing, engineering costs, balancing and/or certifications
- Deck or shell modifications
- Modifications/work to exterior doors, walls, storefront
- Overhead backing of monitors, exam lights or equipment
- High concrete moisture content in existing concrete with associated ramifications or costs associated with remedies
- Permit fees

Clarify and Discuss with Your Contractor
- Help with your budget
- Implementation of Green procedures
- Use of developer's roofer to insure proper workmanship and that the roof remains warrantied
- Verify, provide and install 2" underground conduit needs
- Create and complete your team of professionals
- Schedule all professional services to make sure nothing gets left out
- Proper design of equipment rooms for noise and temperature controls using soundboards, studio foam, properly positioned air supply and thermostatically controlled exhaust
- Verify that the air and vacuum locations/requirements are correct and properly installed
- Provide in-wall backing for future needs as directed by you
- Provide FRP (fiberglass reinforced panels) at equipment room 4' high to ensure durability and longevity
- Guarantee air comfort – air balance your system to your satisfaction
- Use of custom pre-finished stained doors
- When blackout of exterior windows is needed, discuss how it will be best done
- At solid surface tops, include preformed integral sinks
- Aesthetically installed semi-recessed fire extinguisher cabinets
- Concrete pretreat

- Third party plumbing inspections when required
- Provide a 3-stage cleaning of the suite/space: first before equipment install; second before computer install; third and final clean before opening day
- Decide whether to wax or not if waxing of sheet vinyl and VCT prior to equipment installation and again before seeing patients with extra coats of wax.
- Painting is done by roller prior to occupancy to create a beautiful finished and fresh look.
- Discuss when stained concrete is used, include floating the entire floor first to hide all of the unsightly trenches to make sure the finish/look is correct as required in a dental office.
- Clean of windows inside and out.
- Re-key of suite upon completion of construction.
- Closeout manual containing pertinent documents, certifications, material finish selections, construction team information, and extended warranties that Denco stands behind.
- There is more than meets the eye (Items to go over with your Contractor):
    - NICs (Not In Contract)
    - Allowances
    - Formats/Categories
    - True Costs
    - Hidden Costs
    - SF Costs vs. Budget
    - PBO (Provided By Others)

As you can see, it is important to review and clarify not only what is included, but sometimes more importantly the exclusions, to be sure everyone is on the same page.

Remember...

THE FINAL COST OF YOUR OFFICE CAN GREATLY DIFFER FROM LOCATION TO LOCATION.

The final cost will be dependent upon existing conditions, final selections, and the local economy

11
CONTRACTING WITH A GENERAL CONTRACTOR

There are two distinct methods for selecting your building contractor...

COMPETITIVE BIDDING AND NEGOTIATED BIDDING

Competitive Bidding Process

The traditional method in selecting a general contractor is through the competitive bidding process. In this process, the client obtains bids from multiple general contractors (usually 3 or 4 general contractors). This is done by sending a full set of construction documents to each contractor. It is very important that the client and their architect present the project to each contractor fairly and equally.

The purpose of this process is to determine that the client obtains the best price to build the project for a certain time and quality. In order for this process to be successful, the following must be considered:

Pros:

- All contractors need to be pre-qualified to perform the proposed type of project – this is especially important when building a dental office.
- The drawings need to be very detailed and completed.
- All bids need to be compared **carefully** to assure that each contractor's bid is equal to each bidding general contractor.
- You need to feel assured that you are comfortable with each general contractor you invite to bid the project will complete the project as expected and will fulfill all warranty requirements.
- Reassurance that you are getting the best bottom line price

Cons:

- Contractors review plans for loop holes, missing items and areas so their bidding price is less which helps them be awarded the contract.
- Creates a potential adversarial relationship with client
- Since low bidders typically get the project, it can result in multiple change orders.

- Does not allow critical conversations between client, contractor and architect for original intent
- There is typically a more disjointed flow of events because it allows less communication between all parties.
- Details can slip through the cracks.
- Contractors usually exclude costs for items that will be required, such as certain specialty items, by city inspectors, extra inspections, etc. to make bids more competitive.
- Allowances are usually cut to show competitive bids.
- General contractors may use lower quality sub-contractors that are not as qualified to perform the work (time/quality/price) in order to be more competitive.

Risks of Low Bidders

- Will they be in business next year?
- No potential for future warranties
- Subs beat down in price competition result in:
    - Slow response/production
    - Less qualified people on your job
    - Higher incidents of mistakes and accidents
    - Poor quality/substitutions
    - Subs going out of business
    - Less qualified superintendents on the job site
        - Potential risk of sub or general contractor not completing work results in:
    - Subs not paid
    - Lien risks (whereby allowing a person owed money to attach a legal lien on your property until it is paid and/or satisfied)
    - Paying for things twice
    - Project delays
    - Higher change order costs
    - Overall construction time increases

Negotiated Bidding Process

Negotiated work is work that is negotiated between the owner/client and his contractor of choice. Initial plans, if any, are reviewed, details of the project are discussed, and selections such as fixtures and finishes, cabinetry desired, equipment, etc., are made. If costs exceed what the client anticipated, the process of making changes to bring the costs down takes place. This gives the client an active role in deciding what changes are made.

The purpose of this process is to determine that the client obtains the best price for the best quality. In order for this process to be successful, the following must be considered:

General Contractor Responsibilities:
- Must have a defined role in the design process by providing:
    - Preliminary construction cost estimates. These estimates should be performed during the design development phase and should be within 10% of the final estimate (performed after the construction documents are completed.)
    - Construction-scheduling services
    - Assistance in determining the construction methods that will be the best in the current economical environment
- Attend design meetings during the design development and the construction document "Kick-Off" meeting
- Work comfortably with the architect and engineers
- Have an "open book" policy showing the bids to the client and assure that each sub-contractor is qualified
- Have a fixed percentage cost for their fees upfront
- Provide multiple sub-contractor bids for each category for the client review

Pros:
- Negotiated projects allow a client to work with and develop the envisioned dream with a contractor of choice, and ideally the equipment person and lender. This Team spells "success" as it allows the client to benefit fully from all parties' experiences, knowledge and creativity.
- Allows monitoring of costs by all involved parties
- Creates a budget and puts in place a system for cost accountability
- Allows an "open book" process where client and contractor share all costs and quotes received.
- Creates a unified team project building cohesive group of professionals for the ultimate success of the project
- Requires less time for construction

- Typically costs the same as bidding work
- Allows for accountability of all parties
- Allows for open discussion by all parties for cost savings and alternate ways of construction.
- Actively involved from conception to completion and has better understanding of client needs and requirements
- Allows contractor to include items that he knows will be required that are not on the plans
- Allows contractor to help client manage all costs

Cons:

- The client needs to instill trust with their contractor without having costs fixed

"It is unwise to pay too much but it is even more foolish to pay too little."

COMPETITIVE BID VS. NEGOTIATED BID

Which is better for you? Let's take a look...

- **The Competitive Bid**
    - Get The Lowest Price-Not Apples for Apples
    - Many Surprises
    - Substandard Work
    - Exposure to Risks
    - Hidden Issues/ Surprises Not Readily Shared
    - Team Approach Missing
- **The Negotiated Bid**
    - Fixed Mark Up-Get Desired Outcome
    - Work Together- Team Effort
    - Contractor Becomes Advocate for Dentist
    - Requires Less Time for Construction
    - Open Discussions for Cost Saving Opportunities and Manage Costs
    - Contractor Involved from the Beginning
    - Costs the Same…and Usually Less!

A THOUGHT...

If you were to spend $10,000 more for something that you really believe in and *increase your productivity by 25-50%* while *reducing stress* and *saving time*, would approximately $60-120/month* be worth the investment?

*Depending on loan rate.

REMEMBER...

You Get What You Pay For!

12
TIMELINES FOR YOUR PROJECT

COMMON TIME FRAMES

Architecture & Design
- Ground Up: 4 – 8 months
- Tenant Improvement: 1 – 3 months

City Review
- Ground-up: 3 – 12 months
- Tenant Improvement: 1 day to 12 weeks (average 4 weeks)

Interior Finish Selections
(can be completed concurrently with the city review)
- 1 – 8 weeks (Depends on the designer and client involvement and availability.)

Construction
(from once officials found and project started to seeing patients)
- Ground Up: 6 – 12 months
- Tenant Improvements: 2 – 4 months (average 3 months)

Note: A General Contractor will typically not include equipment, IT, set up, training, furnishings, etc., in his schedule.

The average ground up project from start to certificate of occupancy is 18-24 months.

The average tenant improvement from start to certificate of occupancy is 6-8 months

CRITICAL PATH TIMELINE

Client:		Confidential: Y /N
Estimated Shell Completion:		
Move In Deadline:		

Projected Date	Completed Date	Steps To Making the Client's Dream Reality
		1. First mtg with Client; program mtg, gathering info, data, and needs. Attending; Contractor and possibly lender, architect, realtor, equipment specialist.
		2. Meet with lender re: needs/requirements
		3. Meet with realtor; work on needs (renegotiating lease, find new properties, etc.)
		4. Meet with equipment specialist re: needs
		5. Meet with IT re: needs
		6. Client looks at offices and gets down to 2 or 3
		7. Contractor evaluates office(s)
		8. Client selects an office
		9. Negotiations of space
		10. Preliminary drawing(s) mtg and discuss budget(s) with client, architect, contractor, and equipment specialist. Client to work on compilation budget for project to determine financial needs with contractor and other professional assistance
		11. Client count the costs to verify the project will work
		12. Client to sign contract with architect and do a service agreement with contractor so we can provide all information needed for lender
		13. Approve revised floor plan (maybe several mtgs or emails needed to review and approve floor plan prior to this)
		14. Confirm equipment and IT needs; what type of equipment you'll be using in the new rooms and operatories including the ceiling. Confirm chairs, delivery systems, lighting, monitors, etc., type and location, design and finishes client likes
		15. Client mtg with architect and contractor, possibly equip. specialist and IT, to review the floor plan and look at the ceiling and power plan(s). Contractor, equipment specialists, and IT all provide budgets based on all the above information
		16. Architect revise floor, ceiling, and power plan
		17. Client sign off on plans, architect starts engineered and architectural plans
		18. Discuss and work on material finishes and selections. Typically at our first meeting we get 85% selected. We then order a large samples and Schedule a meeting approximately two weeks later to finalize selections
		19. Client approves the material and finish selections
		20. Architectural drawings completed and submitted to the city
		21. Contractor reviews plans and over the course of two weeks get solid numbers and provide final cost breakdown and construction contract to client
		22. Client approves costs and construction contract
		23. Permit obtained
		24. Client to work on: Sign Company, Utility & City Account Set Up, Banners, License, Security
		25. Order and start fire alarm/ fire permit/ gas permit/right of way or other permits required
		26. Review city plans apply all clients final finish selections and decisions and create yellow set of working plans
		27. Equipment ordered
		28. Start construction
		29. Track and make sure all permits in place
		30. One week later, contractor provides timeline to go over with client and discuss transition days, finalize timeline and agree on move in date and critical dates to project
		31. See flow chart of items to consider and work on: Verify business license, power & water accounts are set up, signs, equipment scheduled, finishes complete & fixtures ordered. Order & schedule art, blinds, furniture, phones, computers etc.
		32. 1 month prior to move in. set office team mtg for purpose of scheduling all things that need to be done to move in, with contractor, equip. specialist, IT, office team and client.
		33. Equipment delivery and set up
		34. City finals and C of O
		35. Client set up office, IT
		36. Office training
		37. See patients and enjoy their Dream

©2016 DENCO DENTAL CONSTRUCTION, INC. USED BY PERMISSION.

13
THE FLOW CHART

Projected Date	Actual Date	Project Development	Client Requirements
		1. Introduction/Evaluation Stage · Collect data from client · SF needs evaluation · Needs evaluation form	☐ Hire realtor ☐ Site selection ☐ Demographics of area ☐ Determine needs/programming ☐ Prepare compilation budget ☐ Start financing process ☐ Decide on office/practice philosophy/vision ☐ Create business plan

		2. Decision Stage
		· Preliminary budget
		· Preliminary budget compilation
		· Financial viability
			☐ Financial viability/overhead projections
			☐ Determine equipment needs
			☐ Office/practice philosophy in place
			☐ Lease/purchase negotiations
			☐ Build your own team of professionals:
			    ☐ Lender/ Funding
			    ☐ Dental equipment
			    ☐ Realtor
			    ☐ General contractor
			    ☐ Consultant
			    ☐ Attorney
			    ☐ CPA
			    ☐ IT specialties
			☐ Federal tax ID/employment #'s
			☐ Decide on office theme
			☐ Create office business name
			☐ Begin logo design/branding
			☐ Refine business plan
			☐ LLC name and paperwork in place
			☐ Insurance; disability, business, etc. for loan

		3. Design Stage - Preliminary · Select architect · Design/create floor plan · Confirm budget	☐ Confirm financing ☐ Select equipment ☐ Sign off on design ☐ Decide on basic colors for office ☐ Obtain insurance for property, workman's comp, disability, overhead, liability and malpractice ☐ Finalize and start implementing marketing (i.e., opening soon banner) ☐ Start interview process

Projected Date	Actual Date	Project Development	Client Requirements

		4. Design Stage - Engineering
		· Involve equipment person in design specifications
		· Plans to engineers
		· Colors/finishes for office
		· Decide on specialties required
		· Office name
			☐ Finalize equipment selection/order
			☐ Secure your telephone number
			☐ Decide on office needs:
			    ☐ Appliances
			    ☐ Furniture/artwork
			    ☐ Aquarium/fountain/special design features
			    ☐ Think about staffing needs
			    ☐ Computers/cabling
			    ☐ Dispensers
			    ☐ Telephone
			    ☐ Alarm systems
			    ☐ Specialties
			    ☐ Office consultant needed?
			☐ Submit office name for approval with ADA
			☐ Office/business name in place
			☐ Think about advertising
			☐ Investigate marketing ideas/costs
			☐ Begin compilation of mailing lists
			☐ Business plan in place

		5. Pre-construction Stage · Create firm quote/contract · Engage subcontractors · Subcontractor requirements · Review and sign off on plans · Plans submitted to City for review · Confirm items completed by client · Obtain permit · Verify financing · Preliminary notice · Builders risk in place · Construction schedule · Building access obtained · Project files and Sub agreements made · Confirm suite number with building owner, City and power company	☐ Review/sign off on blueprints ☐ Utility deposits ☐ Telephone system contract ☐ Telephone number secured/forward phone calls to active phone line ☐ "Acquire information on contacts re: building and access ☐ Logo design ☐ Begin designing the storefront sign ☐ Investigate advertising ☐ Visa \ charge card account set up ☐ Security system contract ☐ Network with local business owners
		6. Construction Stage - start · Pre-construction meeting · Demo/sub floor work · Concrete/frame	☐ Licenses ☐ Investigate business and patient insurance ☐ Set up bank accounts ☐ CPA engaged ☐ Work on staffing/interview/select ☐ Advertising plan in place ☐ Order sign/temporary sign ☐ Order business cards ☐ Order stationary/brochures ☐ Mailing lists in place ☐ Office consultant contacted ☐ Network with local business owners ☐ Investigate insurance plans for patients

Projected Date	Actual Date	Project Development	Client Requirements

		7. Construction stage - midway
		· Frame/rough in
		· Rough in
		· Inspections/insulation/drywall
		· Drywall
		· Trim/paint
		· Cabinets/floors/ceiling
			☐ Decide on insurance plans
			☐ Site walk through
			☐ Confirm, telephone, fax, lines and system
			☐ Have a phone number established
			☐ Interview/hire staff
			☐ P.O. Box set up
			☐ Verify utility accounts are set up
			☐ Storefront signage installed
			☐ Client walk through punch list
			☐ Design/set grand opening
			☐ Order Grand Opening banner
			☐ Set up Grand Opening banner
			☐ Free publicity
			☐ Network/meet local dentists
			☐ Set up patient insurance
			☐ Medical Gas account set up and tanks delivered to site week prior to C of O.
			☐ Confirm insurance in place at new location, prior to dental equipment delivery
			☐ Set up credit card processing
			☐ Plan the move/transfer/delivery/install of:
			   ☐ Phones/Security/IT/Cabling/Trim
			   ☐ Confirm power account set/deposit paid
			   ☐ Send out notices to existing patients of new address
			   ☐ Send out marketing/advertising
			   ☐ Order business cards/ letterhead, etc.
			   ☐ City business license in place or update new address on existing/current license
			   ☐ Equipment insurance in place
			   ☐ Appliances, artwork, and furniture ordered and scheduled fordelivery
			   ☐ All equipment ordered and scheduled for delivery
			   ☐ Pack up current office (if relocating)

		8. Construction stage - details
		(one week prior to move)
		· Trim out/details/equipment
		· Details/equipment
		· Certificate of occupancy
		· Client walk through approval
		· Move in
			☐ Confirm all steps from stage 7 are complete
			☐ Client walk through
			☐ Move in, deliver/set up appliances, art, furniture, misc.
			☐ Office consultant information set up/ orientation
			☐ Implement office procedures
			☐ Office training, familiarize team with office
			☐ Osha training
			☐ Free publicity
			☐ Insurance in place
			☐ Have a "test run" day, before opening for business
			☐ Files set up and ready to go
			☐ Items to focus on and make sure are complete:
			☐ Phone setup/transferred
			   ☐ Computer/IT set up
			   ☐ Understand equipment and how to use
			   ☐ Patient process
			   ☐ Payment processes

Projected Date	Actual Date	Project Development	Client Requirements
			☐ Do walk through of office to see how the patient will view the office ☐ Walk through office with team to discuss: 　☐ Create new flow 　☐ New equipment/appliances/thermostat etc., and how to use 　☐ Office maintenance, service, and set up a routine
		9. Construction stage - final · Open for business · Final construction documents · Warranties · Releases · Provide team list/closeout book	☐ Apply for disability credits ☐ Grand opening ☐ Review/evaluate office systems procedures ☐ Day one - schedule light day of patients, to confirm everything works as it should

NOTES:

14
THE BUSINESS MODEL

THE 4 KEYS FOR BUSINESS SUCCESS

1. Client satisfaction = Loyalty
2. Client loyalty generates more powerful referrals to your business…
3. Develop an office design that will:
   - Be efficient for you and your team to provide the highest level of services to your client.
   - Be comfortable and convenient for your clients.
4. Your clients will be "raving fans"!

This model works for your Internal Dental Team and your Dental Office Project Team.

Success Model

The importance of a Solid Business Model

Technology –	**Processes –**
Hardware Software Contiguous Integration	Recordkeeping Workflow Fiduciary Standards
Management –	**Design –**
Employee Production Resources	Branding Functional Office Design

These are the many hats of being a business owner!

SURROUND YOURSELF WITH ACCOUNTABLE PROFESSIONALS MORE KNOWLEDGEABLE THAN YOURSELF.

The Successful Business Model

If everything in your business flows through you and is dependent upon you,

Then you are restricting the growth and profits of your company.

Let's not forget the harm you are doing

To the growth and development of your people.

New Business Structure…How It Looks

If you do not have an effective business system…
YOU ARE THE SYSTEM!

Instead of having a business, you have a glorified job.

You will never escape the technical trenches of your business.

You will always be *"Busy Being Busy."*

Look for A Consultant/Business Coach Who Will Teach You…

- **How to fish rather than catch the fish for you!**
- **The goal of a good consultant should be to work themselves out of a job!**

15
PLANNING THE MOVE

As every dental office is special and unique unto its own, please note that there may be more items to review, discuss or address. This is meant to be an excellent start to plan for your successful move in. For these reasons, we highly recommend that you involve your team in this process.

Date	Prior to Start of Construction
	Logo/Branding/Marketing
	Begin designing the storefront sign
	Start planning for Furniture/Artwork/Appliances, etc.
	Two Weeks After Start of Construction
	Get target dates of completion & finals from contractor and add 2-4 weeks to those dates to schedule move.
	Confirm when equipment needed by G.C. for finals
	Confirm with equipment company date of delivery and install
	Order temporary sign
	Determine how much time you want to allow for moving, set-up, nesting, training, dry runs, etc.
	Plan a comfortable move in date, one everyone can agree to and be accountable to
	Make sure signage is contracted and being made and get banners up ASAP
	Order long lead time items
	Verify all material finish selections have been made and confirmed
	Power accounts set up?
	Plan for a soft opening
	Two Months Prior to Move-In
	Confirm all on target: Contractor, Equipment, Special Equipment
	Advertising plan in place
	Decide On Office Needs-Order/Schedule: ☐ Appliances ☐ Furniture/Artwork ☐ Aquarium/Fountain/Special Design Features ☐ Staffing Needs ☐ Computers/Cabling ☐ Dispensers ☐ Apron Holders ☐ Wall Mount Accessories ☐ Telephone ☐ Alarm System ☐ Specialties ☐ Office Consultant Needed?
	Begin compilation of mailing lists

Date	Four-Six Weeks Prior to Move-In
	Have a blank calendar with dates on one side printed out for the next 45 days and make a copy for each attendee. (Attendees: Doctor, General Contractor, possible key dental team members; IT, specialties and equipment company rep.)

Define critical must-do dates such as:
- ☐ Equipment delivery and install
- ☐ Lease up or current space must be vacated
- ☐ Date seeing first patient
- ☐ When improvement/construction will be done
- ☐ Needs for inspections, 3· party inspections & finals
- ☐ When can deliveries be made
- ☐ When can office be set up
- ☐ Discuss scheduling of everything
- ☐ Schedule new equipment training
- ☐ Block out and schedule required down days for move
- ☐ How long will G.C. provide dumpster on site for your move/garbage/boxes (think donations/recycle)
- ☐ Confirm power and all utilities are on and will not hinder your move in
- ☐ Schedule team w/t of new office to verify all in place. Discuss things missed and new procedures
- ☐ Plan for soft opening and have equipment tech there
- ☐ Schedule with G. C. how to handle punch list and when to do a pre-walk through
- ☐ Determine when med gas tanks to be delivered (if needed)
- ☐ Osha Training

Get moving company quotes
Security system contract
Network with local business owners
Order business cards
Order stationary/brochures
Mailing lists in place
Research moving companies (if needed)
Confirm, telephone, fax, lines and system
Have a phone number established-Need to add lines?
P.O. Box set up
Storefront signage installed
Design Grand Opening Banner/Banners in front
Telephone number posted on banner
Free publicity
Medical Gas account set up and tanks delivered to site week prior to C of O.
Confirm office & equipment insurance in place at new location, **PRIOR** to dental equipment delivery

Plan for the move/transfer/delivery/install of:
- ☐ Banner Opening
- ☐ Phones/Security/IT/Cabling/Trim
- ☐ Note pads for needs
- ☐ Assign Duties/Responsibilities
- ☐ Determine what will go and what will stay
- ☐ Schedule shredding company
- ☐ Prior to the move, advise those who will be handling sensitive equipment and sensors to take extra care
- ☐ Confirm power account set/deposit paid
- ☐ Send out notices to existing patients of new address
- ☐ Send out marketing/advertising
- ☐ Order business cards/ letterhead, etc.
- ☐ Send out notices to Dental offices of your move

Send out notices to all accounts of your address change (credit card, vendor, FedEx, UPS, merchants)
City business license in place or update new address on existing/current license
Appliances, artwork, and furniture ordered and scheduled for delivery
All equipment ordered and scheduled for delivery

Date	Four-Six Weeks Prior to Move-In *(continued)*
	Pack up current office (if relocating)
	Boxes/packing materials
	Insurance plans notified of change
	Specialties, water features, photo room/booth, plants, etc. (Scheduled/Coordinated)
Date	**Two Weeks Prior to Move-In**
	Verify with G.C. and equipment company all is on schedule Schedule/confirm delivery of new items (art, furniture, appliances etc.) Confirm I.T. Box non-needed items (label or color dot boxes) Dentist walk through with team at new office (discuss the move, needs, new procedures) Do job walk with G.C. Client walk thru-punch list Select moving company & schedule Schedule a professional final clean of office prior to move in and again prior to seeing patients Verify equipment company scheduled for disconnect/reconnect Items to focus on and make sure are complete: ☐ Phone setup/transferred ☐ Computer/IT set up ☐ Understand equipment and how to use ☐ Patient process ☐ Payment processes Do walk through of office to see how the patient will view the office Walk through office with team to discuss: ☐ New flow ☐ New equipment/appliances/thermostat etc. and how to use ☐ Office maintenance, service, and set up a routine
	One Week Prior to Move-In
	Confirm with G.C. & equipment company all is on schedule Call phone company regarding line transfer (if needed) Box non-needed items (label or color dot boxes) Install computers/phone system etc. Donation/recycle company called/scheduled Set up new items in office
	One Day Prior to Move-In
	Final Clean of office Finish Boxing, tagging, marking boxes and items to move Confirm moving company
	Day of Move
	Finish boxing, tagging, marking boxes & items to move Transfer phone lines and verify they work Moving company Equipment company out for disconnect/reconnect

	Prior to Seeing Patients
	Verify everything works (computers/phones) Do dry-run of dental procedures/patients
	Day Prior to Opening
	Professional cleaning company does final clean/detail of office
	1st Day Seeing Patients
	Grand Opening Have equipment technician there for first hour or two during soft opening Schedule a light workday as you get used to new surroundings & verify all equipment & processes work.

NOTES:

16
CELEBRATING YOUR OPENING

Celebrate the opening of your new office! First and foremost, it is a celebration of a huge achievement. Pat yourself on the back and acknowledge all you have done.

Other reasons to celebrate include: Acknowledging your significant other, family, friends, colleagues and professionals that have helped make your "Dream a Reality!"

Use this celebration as your opportunity to announce to the neighborhood and the community that you serve to join you and share your commitment, excitement, and beautiful new office. Make sure this celebration portrays who you are and creates new opportunities. Think of your area, others in the complex, or town that may come along side you to create a unique, positive, and impactful event that everyone will remember for years to come!

17
ADDITIONAL HELPS

Common Terms In Lending

Lenders anticipate that the average borrower will generally ask the same question almost every time: "What is your interest rate?" The bottom line is that loans have many variables that should be taken into account in order to make an educated and financially sound decision.

The top three questions asked. Know and understand these as you compare financing options.

1. **What is the rate?**
2. **What are the fees associated with the loan?**
3. **Can I Prepay?**
4. **Terms and definitions**

- **Rate.** Fixed or Variable? When does it lock-in? What is the project-rate versus the permanent financing rate? Is the lock before or after the project, or how many days before closing? And what does it float with during the time that it is not locked? Find out the fixed period of time (that may differ from the payment period or amortization). Find out how the rate is recalculated if the rate period is less than the payment period (prime plus? T-bill plus? LIBOR plus?). Find out the APR (the total annual cost of your loan including fees, rates, and any other charges).

- **Fees.** Front, middle, and back end fees. Are you getting charged for Project Management and if so, how much? There are scores of names for fees including origination fees, documentation fees, packaging fees, appraisal fees, inspection fees, rate-lock fees, franchise fees, commitment fees, etc. Middle fees include fees when re-fixing rates if rate and payment terms don't match. Also, check for items that don't look right and are another way for banks to collect up-front money like Advance Payments. For SBA Lending: Check the SBA Guarantee Fees versus the Banking Fees. Some are required, some are not.

- **Revolving Credit Availability.** Based upon income level, each borrower has a pre-determined amount of accessible credit with all lenders. If too many credit lines are open and accessible to the borrower, his or her ability to secure credit with other lenders and their corresponding credit-rating may be impacted greatly. Also, if credit cards are maxed out, this too can affect their ability to secure credit with other lenders and their corresponding credit rating may be impacted negatively.

- **FICO Score.** FICO stands for Fair Isaac Corporation. This credit rating score can be obtained through the three credit reporting agencies TransUnion, Equifax, and Experian. The credit score is a standard by which a borrower's credit is gauged, and it's determined by use of a mathematical model taking each of the following five areas into account: payment history, current level of indebtedness, types of credit used, length of credit history and new credit. Credit bureaus sell lenders the information so they can assess an applicant's credit risk.

- **Cash Flow Based Lending.** A cash flow based lending decision is founded on the financial feasibility of a given loan request for a specific borrower. This is done by reviewing the practice financials and/or projections to determine the borrower's available net income. The loan payment and borrower's monthly living expenses are then subtracted to determine the bottom line net income. Loan approval is then assessed based upon whether there is sufficient net income or "cash flow" to support the borrower's total financial needs

- **Balance Sheet Based Lending.** A balance sheet based lending decision is founded on offsetting risk in the loan by requiring a borrower to pledge assets as collateral. In doing so, the risk to the lender is mitigated, but the borrower's best interest may not have been fully considered.

- **Vantage Score.** Vantage Score is the credit industry's first credit score developed jointly by Experian, Equifax, and Transunion. This innovative new approach to credit scoring simplifies the credit granting process for consumers and creditors by providing a consistent, objective score to the marketplace. Vantage Score is easy to understand and apply. It uses score ranges from 501 - 990 (FICO is 350 to 850). Consumers and credit grantors alike will recognize the following logical score groupings that approximate the familiar academic scale:

    A: 901 – 990 (Super prime)

    B: 801 – 900 (Prime plus)

    C: 701 – 800 (Prime)

    D: 601 – 700 (Non-prime)

    F: 501 – 600 (High risk)

    A quick way to determine your approximate Vantage Score is to multiply your FICO score by 1.16.

- **Prepayment Penalties.** This is what the lender charges if loan is prepaid. Discuss both prepays: In Whole and In Part. In Whole denotes if you want to pay the entire balance off and want to know any additional costs. In Part refers to making additional payments to principal and pay down the loan more aggressively. Be sure to note the limits of each.

- **Soft Cost Restrictions.** Find out the percentage of your loan that has to be hard equipment. This is a limitation on many loans doctors are sometimes unaware of when they are committing to a lending institution.

- **Term Limitations.** Lenders won't always give you their full term limits unless asked, so ask. Are Graduated payments available? Are Interest-Only payments available? A term is the overall length of the repayment for the loan.
- **Principle.** The principle is the sum of money owed as a debt, upon which interest is calculated.
- **Assets.** An asset is a single item ownership, having exchange or cash value (i.e., - home, cash, portfolio, practice, etc.)
- **Liability.** A liability is an outstanding debt with a corresponding monthly or annual payment obligation. (Liabilities can be either personal or business related.)
- **Point:** A point is a unit equal to 1%, usually an added cost above the quoted interest rate.
- **Fixed vs. Variable Interest Rates.** A fixed rate is one that is held constant over the term stipulated; a variable rate is one that fluctuates based upon the economic indicators, such as prime rate.
- **Collateral.** A loan can be guaranteed by a security pledged against the performance of the obligation; meaning if a borrower does not make their payments, the lender reserves the right to collect on the collateral and sell it to recover the cost of the loan (i.e., practice, real estate, home, etc.)
- **Collateral.** Business only? Personal? Home? Additional Guarantor requirement? If you have an approval, find out what is collateralized with that approval. Am I allowed to have multiple loans? Do I have to finance the entire project with one source? What type of lien are you putting on my practice to collateralize the loan? What payments are due during the project phase?
- **Lender or Broker?** Find out if they are a direct lender or a broker lender. Brokers are a middleman between you and your money and typically have additional fees or higher rates than the direct lender in order to be paid for their services. They are sometimes worth the expense to find an appropriate solution for you, but you want to be aware of their fees or how they get paid.
- **Insurance Requirements.** Life, Disability, and/or Business Property. Find out what amount triggers the need for certain insurance requirements. Find out what percentage of the total balance (for Life), or total payments (for Disability), or amount per operatory (for Business Property) is required. Find out if there are substitute policies acceptable such as Overhead Insurance in place of Disability, or declining term Life Insurance policies that are also acceptable and maybe more appropriate and less expensive.
- **Other Important Terms.** Not just Payment versus Rate terms as suggested above, but terms including approval dates (when does the approval expire? What happens then?), late fee policies, grace periods, and percentage of financing: 80%? 85%? 90%? 100%? Know what it is going into it. Are there carry- backs? What are the terms and restrictions of that?
- **Collateral-based Lender.** Usually a local lender/bank that typically makes credit decisions based on the value of your personal assets and use personal items as such your home, money market accounts and CD's as collateral.

- **Cash Flow Lenders.** Usually specialty lenders that focus on a particular industry/business model and use the historical performance of a practice – or, in the case of start-ups, projected revenue and cash flow – to make credit decisions and use the practice as collateral, not your personal assets.
- **Credit.** Is this a business loan or does this report personally? How does that work? READ YOUR APPROVALS. Make sure first of all it is an actual approval and not a prequalification or pre-approval. Then read the terms and conditions of that approval carefully and fully to make sure what they are asking for is available and acceptable. An approval with unattainable conditions is a decline.

COMMERCIAL REAL ESTATE FINANCING

Once you have determined whether you will build a ground up, buy, remodel, lease a space, or do a tenant improvement, you will need to secure your financing.

If you build or purchase a new office, you will need to secure long-term funding. Two types of financing are available:

- **Conventional Loans** – typically require a set period of time that you have owned and operated a business with up to 30% down.
- **SBA Loans** – (Small Business Administration) loans are designed to help new businesses get started. They typically have lower down payment requirements, longer repayment terms, and have competitive rates.

    Note: If choosing an SBA lender
    - Choose a "Preferred SBA Lender" and one that is familiar with the SBA lending process.
    - Also note some lenders will work together with "competitors" to provide the balance of funding of up to 100% of the desired loan. So ask.

HOW TO IMPROVE PATIENTS' ACCEPTANCE OF TREATMENT

Most Important Things in your Dental Practice:

- Honesty
- Dentistry
- Personality
- Staff impressions
- Office appearance
- Location

What is the order of importance?

1. Personality
2. Honesty
3. Dentistry
4. Office appearance
5. Staff impressions
6. Location

What's missing?

...Service!

The dentist's ability is important, but in the business world, not as much as the other factors!

Reduce the stress on the patient and you!

- Introduction – welcome
- Connect – open ended questions/touch
- Ask why they are here today
- Listen!
- Educate, show x-ray
- Provide options with understanding – use intraoral camera, explain, provide options A, B, C, etc. with pros and cons by looking on the screen
- They choose
- Wait for response – Wait! Wait! Wait!
- They own it!
- Positive results – higher case acceptance with fewer no shows

HOW *NOT* TO IMPROVE PATIENTS ACCEPTANCE

Worst Question to Ask...

"What's stopping you from getting this done today?" No Support

- No inner oral photograph
- Patient not shown x-rays/pictures

If Patient does not own the problem
- High percentage of no shows
- They increase chance of not coming back

If Patient still does not own the problem and Dental work is completed
- A problem occurs now or in the future… whose fault or problem has it become?

OTHER WAYS TO IMPROVE DENTISTRY AND YOUR INCOME

- Listen to your patients.
- Build relationships with patients.
- Market your practice.
- Build trust with patients.
- Sit in your exam chair to see and experience what your patients do.
- Walk in and through your office, as a new patient, would you come here? Do you like what you see?
- Look at your issues, list them, prioritize and work on the top one or two that will give you the biggest return.
- Stop trying to do it all yourself.
- Does your office denote the type of dentistry that you do?
- Stop decision paralysis. Usually happens when a dentist gets too many suggestions.
- Invest in your practice.
- Do what you do best …dentistry!

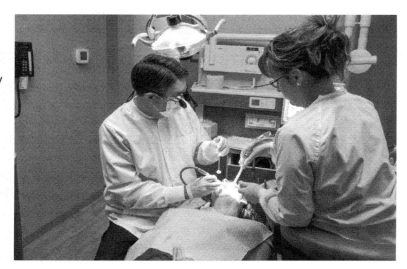

How Do You Obtain Highest Rate of Return for Dental Office Investments Toward Your Future?

Out-Source Work You Don't Enjoy:

Do What You Are Good at…

…then Hire Professionals for the Rest!

- Payroll by Professionals

- Marketing
- Office Improvements…Minor to Major or New
- Technology
- CPA/ Planner Who Understands Dental!
  Provided by Steve Owens (Owens and Bondell)

I Have Experienced:

- Simply painting, cleaning up, and installing new flooring can **increase your productivity by 6%!**
- Doing a major renovation or new office will increase **your productivity an average of 20% the first year.**
- Too many dentists wait to remodel and update their office, usually waiting until they are tired and worn out. When they do remodel **we often see a dentist change their mind and want to continue dentistry.**

STRESS POINTS FOR A DENTIST

- Staff
- Patients
- Self
- Appearance of office
- Personal life

Personal Assessment

- Be honest with yourself.
- Problems? What are they?
- If so, am I the cause?
- Fix the problem(s).
- Get qualified professionals that know how to do their job.
- Let the professionals DO their job – do not micro-manage.
- Rise to the top.
- Develop a team mentality.

Assessing Your Team – (Not Staff):
- I have them work with me, not for me.
- Hire staff that can do it better than I can.
- Put people around me that are smarter in their field than I am.
- If they cannot do the job, quickly assess and get rid of them.

Are You a Prisoner of Your Own Business?

Your business should not depend upon
- Your presence
- Personality
- Problem solving
- For its daily survival
- If so, your business does not work…you do!
- You will always remain a prisoner to your own business.

Team Acknowledgment:
- Everyone on the team is of equal importance
- Leave your ego in the trash can
- Regularly acknowledge the team and their importance
- Compliment the team especially in front of the patient
- Treat the team how you would like to be treated
- Everyone on the team is your equal (you write the check and make major decisions and that is it!)
- Involve team on office decisions, listen and apply where and when possible
- Create team building experiences

Dental Office Assessment

- Give great service, great service, and more great service.
- Happy office atmosphere…have fun in the office!
- Do not have a serious attitude all of the time.
- This is not brain surgery or life or death…be nice to everyone: team, patients, and everyone in your life!

18
OFFICE MAINTENANCE

Suggested Maintenance Schedules For Dental Offices

See below for a general list of equipment items (some may not apply to your office as this is just a general guide) and the suggested intervals in which they should be serviced. We recommend reviewing this with your equipment company to confirm and adjust to your specific office needs.

Daily:

At the beginning of the day:

- Turn on compressor, vacuum and main water solenoid lines.
- Check fluid levels in sterilizer and x-ray processor (topping off if necessary) and then turn them on. Run a cleaning sheet through your processor (if such is available for it).
- Turn on delivery systems and open oxygen and nitrous tanks (if you have a central system). Check ultrasonic cleaner solution.
- If using self-contained water systems and air purging every night, run hand pieces and depress water buttons on air/water syringes to establish water line pressure.
- Refill water bottles of self-contained systems.
- Verify previous day's computer back-up and install next generation of media (i.e. the next drive/cartridge etc. in sequence).

At the end of the day:

- Clean the sterilizer door gasket with a soft cloth and mild (non-antibacterial) liquid soap.
- Clean out or change chairside vacuum traps and run vacuum system cleaner through all vacuum lines. Be certain to securely replace the lid of the trap after checking screen on trap.
- Empty waste bottle/tank on sterilizers equipped with one.
- Turn off all equipment as above – delivery systems, oxygen and nitrous tanks, sterilizer, processor, compressor, vacuum, and main water line. If using a Dent-X processor, remove the cover and slide the covers of the solution trays to the side allowing vapors to escape.
- Dry water lines by purging with air (if using self-contained water systems).

Weekly:

Dental Air Compressor - Check moisture indicator

Clean interior and exterior of sterilizer(s), including reservoir. Check autoclave safety valve by pulling on the ring with pliers (it should spring back).

Check sterilizer filters and perform a spore test. Verify sterilizer is level.

Check chairside trap screens and lid O-rings for wear and replace if necessary. Be certain to securely replace the lid of the trap afterward.

Check and replace or clean out central vacuum and main water line filters. Check amalgam separator (if present).

Disassemble and lubricate vacuum valves (HVE and SE). Clean ultrasonic cleaner.

Clean operating light reflectors and lens shields (make sure reflectors are cool first).

Check oil on oil-lubricated compressors and drain compressor tank. An auto-drain can also be installed on your compressor to drain as needed automatically.

Clean processor racks according to manufacturer's instructions. You may need to let them dry over the weekend as well.

Empty and clean out bottles of self-contained water systems. Clean boiling chamber of water distiller

Monthly:

Perform extended cleaning of x-ray processor per manufacturer's recommendations. Special cleaning solution may be required as well.

Check/clean plaster trap

Check emergency resuscitation equipment

Lubricate joints in operating lights, sterilizer door hinges, air/water syringe buttons, & other similar items around the office.

Clean Pan or Ceph x-ray screens with a screen cleaner.

Using heat-resistant PPE, check sterilizer safety valve while under pressure (see Sterilizer Maintenance) & check sterilizer door for plumb.

Check air and water filters in junction boxes.

Quarterly:

Vacuum Lines - Check gear lube level in sealed gearbox Check filters on compressor and central vacuum.

Check compressor oil (if oil lubricated)

Check tubing on delivery systems, nitrous, and vacuum as well as hand piece gaskets and/or coupler O-rings for signs of wear.

Check/clean plaster trap

Clean model trimmer wheel and drain lines. Lubricate drive chain on Dent-X processors. Check hydraulic fluid of patient chair.

Check life of computer battery back up (UPS). Test smoke alarms.

Verify computer back up by restoring from a back up.

Biannually:

Dental Air Compressor – Replace exhaust muffler HVAC Units -

Preventive Maintenance/Pre-Season Maintenance

Replace air filter every 90 days but check it monthly. If its dirty, replace it!

Annually:

Backflow Preventers RO Systems

Dental Air Compressors

Replace air intake filters/Replace air filter element and O-Ring.

Vacuum Lines – Belt/Tank

Change sterilizer door gasket, bellows and fill filters.

Change oil (if oil lubricated) of compressor.

Check power cords for all electronic equipment around the office and replace any that are frayed or worn.

Have fire extinguisher(s) inspected.

Observe a complete sterilization cycle looking for any signs of malfunction such as a steam leak. Conduct staff OSHA training

Review emergency procedures with staff- how to handle patient emergencies as well as what to do in case of fire etc.

Have X-ray equipment inspected, calibrated, and certified (requirements vary may be as infrequently as once every 5 years)

In General:

Be observant. Note any equipment that exhibits unusual behavior such as loud or abnormal noises or an unusual appearance/discoloration.

Keep owner's manuals for all equipment in a secure place.

Consult owner's manuals for manufacturer's recommended maintenance and supplement the list above accordingly.

Check with local authorities for your requirements. Some things (for example spore tests) may have a different frequency requirement in your area. We have attempted to list such things at the most common interval but there can be wide variation. Be aware of seasonal tendencies for extremes of heat, cold, & humidity and the effect these extremes can have on specific pieces of equipment. For example, replacing compressor dryer desiccant is commonly required in the summer months.

It may be helpful to have primary equipment wired to a master switch to simplify turning on in the morning and off at night (just one switch to throw).

Be mindful of critical equipment and always have spares of the following on hand:

- Light bulbs for operating lights and curing lights
- Filters for air and water lines
- Replacement screens/traps for central vacuum
- Fuses for chairs, sterilizer, processor, etc.
- Hydraulic fluid (if you have hydraulic chairs)
- Compressor oil
- Have a back-up plan in case of failure of compressor, vacuum or sterilizer. Having a smaller secondary unit on hand that can be "hot-swapped" temporarily. This can keep you up and running.
- Have a contingency plan in case of computer system failure.

As stated previously, this list should not be considered all-inclusive and there will be variations depending on what equipment you use. Please take time to confirm with your equipment company which of the above items and possible others that apply to you.

19
CASE STUDIES

The section below is for lectures and seminars when Steve shows his slide presentation.

1. CREATING A TRUSTED TEAM:

- **No Trusted Team**
    - Poor floor plan
    - Lots of unrealized dreams
    - Numerous design problems
- **Started Trusting Individuals**
    - Still no team
    - Great floor plan, not full trust
    - Not allowing all to talk or see the site
- **Trusting the Team**
    - All team together
    - Visit site
    - Fixed problems
    - Joint effort to success

"Denco was always open minded towards changes proposed during construction."

– Dr. Rodney Palmer

2. Progressive Growth

- **First Office**
    - Existing vacated dental office
    - Location
    - $40k in T.I.'s
    - $250k school debt
- **Second Office**
    - 2 years later
    - $100k school debt

- Moved/tore down old office
- Location
- $225K in T.I.'s
- **Transition**
    - 3 years later
    - No school debt
    - Desire to own/invest
    - Purchased land close-by
- **Third Office**
    - 2 years later
    - Sold land – made $100k
    - Bought building
    - Location
    - $500k in T.I.'s
    - Money in bank

3. Refinance/Expansion: 2400 SF, 6 Ops, $125k/Op.

- **The Status:**
    - $125k/Op.
    - Room to grow
    - Add associates
- **The Reality:**
    - 78% utilization
    - Use practice equity
- **New Choices:**
    - New technology
    - Improved efficiencies
- **The Decision of New Space:**
    - Growth
    - Excited Doctor
    - Excited staff
- **The Options:**
    - Rates fixed

- Lower rates
- Interest rate savings
- Locked in projected rates
- **The Results:**
  - New experience
  - New practice
  - New energy
  - Cash flow
  - At or better than current reality

"Throughout all three of my dental offices, Denco made sure there was always open communication."

Dr. Rodney Palmer

4. The Cost Of Choices: Inexperienced Architect & Contractor:

To save $5K in architectural/engineering fees

- **Unnecessary costs:**
  - Preliminary space planning took 2 months longer
  - Having to delete plans for additional building square footage
  - Later found insufficient parking issues
  - Took them 14 months to move in!
  - An additional $60K in mortgage fees
  - Additional rent he has to pay at 150% at his current space!
  - Loss of productivity due to poor flow and design!

5. Client Design And The Cost Of A Cheap Bid:

- **What Happened:**
  - The client received and accepted a lower lump sum "bid"
  - Bid was from an inexperienced general contractor
  - General contractor had little experience in dental construction
  - Bid had no specifications on what they had included/excluded

- **The Results:**
    - Unacceptable construction
    - Time delays
    - Missed opening
    - Did not know/understand vacuum/ air/ and op. needs
    - Numerous change orders
    - Contractor refused to do corrective work
    - Law suit; lengthy and expensive litigation

6. Investing In The Right Equipment:

Drs. Slepak and Goyal saw the need for improving technology in their office

- **His investment initially was**
    - A Cone beam
    - A Cerec
    - With concern… "How do we pay for it?"
- **Within Six Months His Office**
    - Benefited his practice in many ways
    - Technology increased production exponentially
    - Opened doors to new options for them
    - Will allow opening a new dental office within 12 months with another Cerec and milling machine priority of technology in the new office

"Our increased production quickly showed us the need for a new larger office with more technology."

Dr. Alexander Slepak

7. Two Dentists And An Unknown Future:

- Inexperienced dental architect drew the original design from the dentists ideas
- The office has one left and one right-handed dentist
- Denco revised the floor plan and provided options and worked with the architect

8. Importance Of A Clear 5-Year Plan!!!

- Asked hard questions
- Better zoning and flow
- Less wasted space
- Created a high volume/easily run office

9. Success Of Extreme Relocation:

"My referrals increased because the visibility and ease of finding the office, along with an office I now can be proud of. Morale in the office has also increased. My team and I really enjoy coming to work in the new office."

Dr. John Wood

"I made the move and right away, I noticed a 12% increase just by making the move. My production increased by having a better flowing design and advancement of technology."

Dr. John Wood

10. Proper Team Alignment In Early Stages:

- Early evaluation found the need for fire sprinklers
    - Landlord paid for it
    - Saved $30K to client

"Since opening, we have had 300 new patients in approximately six weeks!"

Sherry Scott

11. Iconic Branding Design:

- The value
- The importance
- The rewards

"Denco completed our office several weeks before the contract date and beyond my expectations. In addition, the overall quality and attention to detail was excellent."

Dave White

12. Successful Remodel While Operating:

"I continually brag to patients that we were able to maintain four operatories while doubling our square footage and never missed one day of scheduled work. I don't know of anyone else who has doubled their office capacity in their existing suite and was able to keep their doors open the entire time."

Dr. Kevin Rauter

20
WRAP UP

How to Prepare for a New Office:

1. Save money
2. Determine your vision/goals
3. Select your team and share your vision/budget/needs
4. Prequalification for a loan
5. Select the site
6. Determine equipment/IT/special needs
7. Design the space
8. Count the cost: Revisit vision/budget/needs.
9. Evaluate objectively
10. Complete architectural plans/permit.
11. Finishes/other team members & functions/revisit budget
12. Construction proves/equipment move in
13. Celebrate your opening

"Remember – it is all about you and your dream!"
– Steve Anderson

Action Points:

- Surround yourself with a team more knowledgeable than yourself that looks out for your interests.
- Put your dream on paper/create a business plan.
- Share it with a significant other – be in agreement.
- Confirm that you are meant to be an owner.
- Count the cost!
- Be yourself… not someone else.

WHAT DO YOU THINK ABOUT THESE TREES?

What Sets These Trees Apart?

- They Shed Their Dead Weight!
- Lose What They Do Not Need!
- They Have A Deep Root System!
- If Burned Or Cut Down They Come Back Multifold!
- Wind And Nature Strengthen Them!
- They Reach For The Stars!

AND SO CAN YOU!

Making Your Dream a Reality!

WHAT OUR CLIENTS SAY

"You did an amazing job and I'm so grateful!"

— Dr. Allison House

"This dental office, built from the slab up, required special attention. Denco made it happen with grace and precision. Working with Denco was an absolute pleasure. The construction schedule developed by Denco…progressed right on schedule…and was completed within the target week with perfect execution and leadership. You will not find a better group of **professional, honorable, and dedicated** people than at Denco."

— Dr. Alexander Slepak

"At our final walk-thru Steve asked one question: "Would you do anything different?" My answer was clear immediately. I would not change one thing about how our project went. No details were overlooked. **Denco builds dental practices. Their expertise is clear.** Our patients and staff love our new office."

—Synergy Dental

"**You made it happen when I thought it could not be done!**"

— Dr. John Harman

"Very happy with the end result! Good subs, great working relationships. **A solid project, a very positive experience.** Gary Takacs is happy with the design and project."

—Dr. Paul Nielson

"Our patients continually compliment the new space and our employees are proud to come to work each day. **It was a great experience** and it makes me confident to use you again for future construction projects."

—Dr. Rodney Gold

"Steve Anderson runs an exceptional company. Our finished building is gorgeous. We have received innumerable compliments on the high quality of craftsmanship. We have been impressed not only with the outstanding results, but also with the fact that every project was completed on schedule. Any minor issue that has come up has been resolved quickly. Out of all the people we worked with, **Denco's service and quality work shines high above all the rest.** Steve Anderson, the president, personally helped resolve some of the headaches and problems that we've had with other companies."

—Dr. Curtis Johnson and Dr. Scott Larsen

"**There were no surprises with Denco Dental Construction.** They performed as they said they would…no extras were added to the project."

—Dr. Rick Jacobi

"Denco Dental Construction did an outstanding job on constructing my new dental office…[Y]our entire team…was extremely professional, courteous and fair with us. Further you **met every deadline**, even completing the office on your exact projected finish date…I truly think you as the 'dream team' that built our 'dream office'. I cannot thank you enough."

—Dr. Kelly Hilgers

"Steve did my office over 13 years ago and when it came time to do my new office, I knew that at least one thing was final-no bids, no agonizing over fine print, referrals, etc. etc. I called Steve up and told him I was planning to build and he was **the man to do it!** Steve was **always available with advice and help on everything from plans to selections through the entire building project.** Our project got completed on schedule and within the expected budget!"

—**Dr. Urvi Dave**

"Steve worked well with my architect, interior designer and myself to solve unique challenges my project posed and **never said 'it can't be done.'**"

—**Dr. Blair Feldman**

"Phone calls are returned promptly…you are **a pleasure to work with…always felt that we were number one on your list.** Thanks for the continual updates, input, suggestions, flexibility with my indecisiveness, advice and professionalism. I can't tell you how much it meant to me when you insisted that things were done right."

—**Dr. Troy Christensen**

"**Work was done professionally and efficiently** while remaining on schedule and within our projected budget."

—**Dr. Rodney Palmer**

"I'd like to thank you for standing behind your work after 2.5 years. **Denco's reputation was the reason I chose your company in the first place.** By helping us fix the sprinkler problem, you've justified my choice when I built my practice. Please continue to serve the dental community well."

— **Dr. Glen Bui**

"I am just so appreciative of how easy you guys are to work with. **You really do go above and beyond for the client even after the job is done.** Please feel free to have new/potential clients call me on my cell phone, I am always happy to discuss the service I received from Denco!"

—**Sherry Scott with Cute Smiles**

"I just wanted to send a note of gratitude and appreciation for the wonderful work you ALL did for us before, during and after the construction of our new office. I came into this project with a lot of questions and worries about budget, timelines and quality and you guys nailed all three areas. You finished on time (on a tight schedule for sure), on budget and the quality was apparent throughout the whole project. **We are glad we did our homework and found you guys!**"

—**Dr. Christopher Drew**

"Steve and his Team went over every little detail. One of the things I appreciate the most was that I was listened to. They did more than build me an office. **They took my vision and dreams and turned it into reality.**"

— **Dr. Nathan McLaws**

"**Your knowledge and expertise in the dental field is rare** and you proved that to us through and through. Your involvement in the design and construction process helped us to achieve the office that we had envisioned."

—**Dr. J. Anthony Ryu**

"Steve Anderson is **professional, knowledgeable and honest.** He made sure that whatever the office needed, it was taken care of. From the initial meeting to the final punch list, he made the whole process smooth and painless."

— **Dr. Toby VanLandschoot**

"From my first phone call I was impressed with your professionalism and thoroughness. It was great to work with you and your competent team. **We get compliments daily about how comfortable and unique our office is.**"

— **Dr. Steven Call**

"**What sets Denco apart are their "can do" attitude, organizational skills, integrity, and honesty.** Not only is Steve a true, honorable professional, but he has become a friend in the process as well."

— **Dr. Tyler Carter**

"Steve Anderson makes a real effort to give his client the things he wants in an office and beyond. He is creative in his designs, makes excellent suggestions when they are needed and does what he says he will do. **Denco's quality of work is excellent and went beyond my expectations.**"

— **Dr. John G. Wood**

"**I was really happy with every facet of the process with you.** You run your business the way I run mine. Number one concern is always make sure the customer (patient) is happy! Great Job!"

— **Dr. Michael Beckham**

"I would like to thank you for building me a wonderful new office. It was the smoothest construction project I have ever been a part of. Your future clients can be comfortable about **your ability to run a professional, caring project that was totally on budget and finished ahead of schedule.**"

— **Dr. Michael Grams**

"We are writing in reference to your superb workmanship in helping us create our dental office. From the pre-construction phase…to the final stages, we were pleased with your attention to detail and timeliness. You and your team were **diligent in allowing us to have a dental office that was beyond our expectations.**"

— **Dr. Michelle Villanueva and Don Fernandez**

"I wanted to officially thank you for doing such a great job with the office…you went **way beyond what my expectations were**. You built me what I consider to be the premier dental office in Arizona. If anyone ever has any doubts, just send them to my office to look first hand at the results."

— **Dr. Brian Allmendinger**

WHAT LENDERS HAVE TO SAY ABOUT DENCO

"Compass Bank values our working relationship with Denco. Having worked on many jobs together, **we are so confident about Denco's excellence in every area, that we have waived many of the requirements we typically place on contractors during the initial loan process**. We look forward to working with Denco on many upcoming projects".

—**Compass Bank SBA Lending - Jim Hunter**

"Bank of America has worked with Denco on multiple jobs. We have established a great working relationship and have **found Denco to meet and often exceed in every area of the construction loan process**."

—**Bank of America Practice Solutions - Scott Mueller**

"Denco Dental Construction, Inc. has worked with Wells Fargo on many jobs and has maintained an excellent track record in providing all necessary requirements for the construction loan process. Denco has **proven time and again to provide thorough records and follow through on every job**."

—**Wells Fargo Small Business Lending - Joseph Giordano**

"Denco has been added to our "Circle of Gold" for Contractors. They have always met our requirements so well and in such detail in fact that we have waived many of our restrictions for them. **We know when we deal with Denco, everything is in order**."

—**CIT Small Business Lending - Kimberly Hellweg**

"From the first time we worked with Denco it was clear they knew their way around the construction loan industry. **It is a pleasure to work with a company that is so well versed in this arena**."

—**Ironstone Bank - Rick Clements**

"Just finished working on your final pay app for Dr. Rodney Gold. You are sharp. The most professional, complete project I've ever had to work through. And no Payment Voucher. **You're a model GC.** Or maybe it's the Finance/Contract Administrator…anyway, Awesome job! Thanks."

—**Lenders Quality Assurance, Mike Mart**

SPECIAL THANKS

I have so many people to thank that I may inadvertently miss some names, but I will never forget each of their contributions. I want to express my sincere thanks to my wife Debbie, my family and each person mentioned below that helped knowingly and unknowingly with their professional thoughts, insights, creativity and support, without whom this book would not be a reality.

Arizona Dental Association	Beverly Giardino
Carrie Agle	Fred Heppner
Darlene Agle	Rick Jacobi, DDS
Debbie Anderson	J.R. Jiminez
Eric Anderson	Chris Kaufman
Jennifer Anderson, DNP	Tony Kong
Michael Anderson	John Lighthizer
Rich Andrus	Ann Lorenger
Jay Baer	Tanner Milne
Shane Bennett	Steve Owens
Steve Blanchette	Casey Potash
Wendee Bren	Dave Rosas
Linda Brennan	David Rinkes
Grant Call	Nick Rulli
Curtis Carter	Lindsey Springfield
Sarah Cottingham	Kristen Thayer
Rhonda Crispin	Chris Torregrossa
Amy Deschamps	Jeremy Tuber
Kevin Earle	Scott Wunderlich
Marty Fifer	Terry Xelowski
Dan Foley	Phyllis Yancy

ALONG WITH THE ENTIRE DENCO DENTAL CONSTRUCTION, INC. TEAM

Making Your Dream a Reality!

ABOUT STEVE ANDERSON

AUTHOR & PRESIDENT OF DENCO DENTAL CONSTRUCTION, INC.

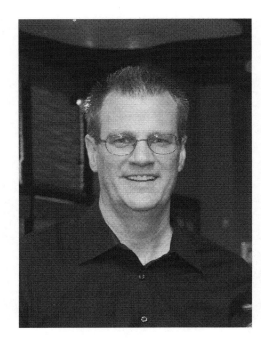

President of Denco Dental Construction, Inc.

General contractor **for over 30 years, specializing in dental offices for nearly 20 years**

Rated A+ by the Better Business Bureau

The *only* General Contractor **endorsed by the Arizona Dental Association!**

Responsible for the construction of over **five hundred** dental offices!

Expert in all aspects of dental office construction, including flow/design review, analysis of contracts, and lease review recommendations

Regular Speaker at Arizona Dental Schools; A.T. Still University, Midwestern University, and the Arizona School of Dentistry & Oral Health

Guest Speaker at 2010 and 2013 Western Regional Dental Convention "Dental Office Design Construction Seminar"

Author of *A Dentist's Blueprints to Success*, the resource for dental office construction

Author of "Another Dream Come True…"

Author of "Tidbits for Success"

Married 38 years to Debbie Anderson. Proud parents to Eric, Michael, and Jennifer. Proud grandparents of Hannah and Keenan, and great-grandparents of Braydon.